FOUNDATIONS OF HISTORY

Russia and the USSR 1905–1956

JANE SHUTER

Heinemann

Heinemann Library

Halley Court, Jordan Hill, Oxford OX2 8EJ
a division of Reed Educational & Professional
Publishing Ltd

OXFORD MADRID ATHENS FLORENCE PRAGUE
CHICAGO PORTSMOUTH NH (USA) MEXICO CITY
SAO PAULO SINGAPORE KUALA LUMPUR TOKYO
MELBOURNE AUCKLAND IBADAN NAIROBI
KAMPALA GABORONE JOHANNESBURG

First published 1996

00 99 98 97 96
10 9 8 7 6 5 4 3 2 1

British Library Cataloguing in Publication data
is available from the British Library on request.

ISBN 0431 058369 (P/b 0431 058377) 947.84

Produced by Dennis Fairey & Associates Ltd
Illustrations by Arthur Phillips
Printed by Mateu Cromo in Spain
Cover design by Ron Kamen
The publishers would like to thank Dr Stephen Vickers
and Andy Harmsworth for their comments on the
original manuscript.

Acknowledgements
The publishers would like to thank the following for
permission to reproduce photographs:

Bettmann Archive: 51
Centre for the Study of Cartoons and Caricature: 57
Jean-Loup Charmet: 16 below
Edimedia: 61
Hoover Institute: 18, 20, 25, 36, 37, 42, 48, 53, 59
Hulton Deutsch: 27, 29 centre
David King: 5, 10, 14, 21, 26, 40, 44, 56
Mansell Collection: 46
Radio Times/Hulton: 39
Roy Miles Gallery, London: 43 below
Novosti: 6, 16 top, 23, 29 left, 43, 49
Society for Co-operation in Russian and Soviet Studies:
    29 right
Times Newspapers Limited/Michael Powers: 31
Topham Picture Library: 7

Details of written sources
In some sources the wording or sentence structure has
been simplified to ensure that the source is accessible.

N. Adeev, *Revolution in 1917: A Soviet Chronicle*,
London, 1923-7: 4.1B, 4.3L
Alexander Barmine, *One Who Survived*, Putnam, 1945: 5.4F
J. Brooman, *The Great War*, Longman, 1992: 3B
J. Brooman, *Stalin and the Soviet Union*, Longman, 1992: 7.1B
Meriel Buchanan, *Dissolution of an Empire*, John Murray,
    1937: 3C, 4.2H

Brian Catchpole, *A Map History of Russia*, Heinemann, 1974: 2
Deutscher and King, *The Great Purges*, Blackwell, 1984: 6.4X
M.T. Florinsky, *The End of the Russian Empire*, Putnam, 1971:
    3.1/1
David Floyd, 'Russia 1905-12', *History of the Twentieth Century*
    Purnell, 1974: 2.5 6
Peter Gilliard, *Thirteen Years at the Russian Court*, London,
    1921: 2.4H
Eugenia Ginzburg, *Into the Whirlwind*, Collins, 1981: 6.4W
Joan Hasler, *The Making of Russia*, Longman, 1968: 7.1C
G. Katkov, *Russia 1917*, Longman, 1967: 3.1/7
Alexander Kerensky, *The Catastrophe*, New York, 1927: 4.2A
Alexander Kerensky, *Russia and History's Turning Point*,
    1965: 1.1D
John Laver, *Lenin, Liberator or Oppressor?*, 1994: 5.6/6/7
Letters of the Tsarina to the Tsar, 1914-16, introduction
    by Sir Bernard Pares, London, 1923: 2.4I, 4.1A
Lenin, Vladimir Ilich, *Collected Works*, Vols. 44 and 45,
    Lawrence and Wishart, 1970: 5.3B, 5.4J
Lenin, Vladimir Ilich, *Testament*: 6.1B, 6.1C
R. Medvedev, *Khrushchev*, 1982: 7.1E
Brian Moynahan, *The Russian Century*, Random House,
    1984: 5.4K
New York Tribune, December 1918: 4.5/5
J.E. O'Connor, *The Sokolov Investigation*, Souvenir Press,
    1972: 4.5/2/3/4
Richard Pipes, *The Russian Revolution 1899-1918*,
    Collins Harvill, 1990: 2.4G, 3.1/2, 5.2A
John Robottom, *Russia in Change 1870-1945*, Longman,
    1984: 6.3L, 7.3/3
J. Scott, *Behind the Urals*, Houghton Mifflin, 1942: 6.2K
Alexander Solzhenitsyn, *The Gulag Archipelago*,
    Harvill Press, 1974: 6.2I
Stalin, Josef, *History of the Communist Party of the Soviet Union*,
    1939: 6.4T
Stalin, Josef, *Selected Writings*, Greenwood Press,
    1942: 6.2E, F, 6.3N
M. Szeftel, *The Russian Constitution of April 23, 1906*,
    Brussels, 1976: 2.4D
The Times, 10 July, 1993: 4.5/7
Trotsky, Leon, *History of the Russian Revolution*, Pluto,
    1977: 5.4E, 5.4G
Trotsky, Leon, *My Life: An attempt at an Autobiography*,
    Pathfinder, 1970: 4.3J
Alan White, *Russia and the USSR*, Collins, 1994: 6.3P
de Witte, Sergei, *Memoirs of Count de Witte*,
    edited by Abraham Yarmolinsky, London, 1921: 2.4E
R.E. Zelnik, translator, *A Radical Worker in Tsarist Russia*,
    1986: 1.1B

CONTENTS

CHAPTER 1

RUSSIA UNDER THE TSAR

1.1 What was Russia like in 1905?

In 1900, the Russian Empire (usually called Russia) took up a sixth of the world's surface. The **Tsar** ruled Russia. Most Russians believed that God chose the Tsar's family (the Romanovs) to rule. Russia was big, but it was not a rich country. The Tsar's family and the **nobles** (who owned most of the land) lived a life of luxury. But most Russians were poor **peasants** or factory workers. Opposition to the Tsar was growing.

▼ The Russian Empire in 1905.

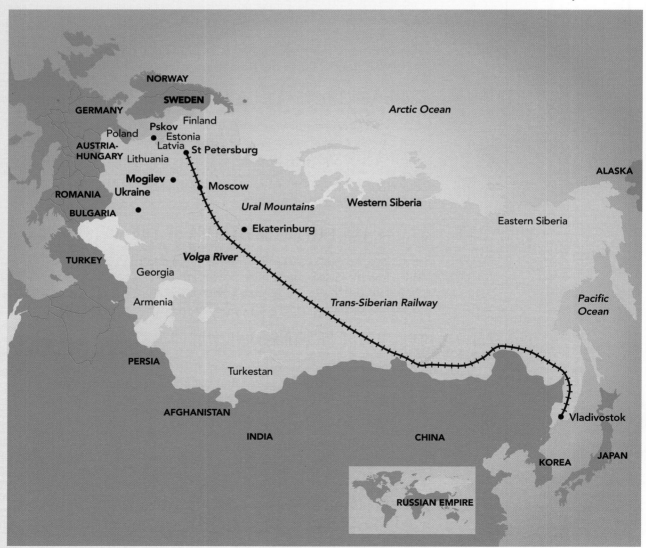

◀ A Russian village in about 1900.

A huge Empire

In 1905, Russia was almost one hundred times the size of Britain. It stretched from Europe in the west to the Pacific Ocean in the east, from the Arctic Ocean in the north to Afghanistan in the south. Its size made it almost impossible to govern. Road travel was slow and difficult, especially in the winter. Even the new **Trans-Siberian Railway** took weeks to cross the country.

An ungovernable people?

The Russian Empire was not one united country. It was a collection of very different people with the same ruler. Less than half of the 125,000,000 people in the Russian Empire were Russian. There were over 100 different nationalities who spoke different languages and had different religions. They had different ways of life, too, adapted to the widely different climates, from the frozen north to the sunny south. They did not feel part of one nation. Many wanted to break away from Russia and rule themselves.

Life in the countryside

In 1900, over three-quarters of Russians were peasants. Much of Russia's farmland was of poor quality. The peasants found it hard to feed the growing population. Food shortages were common. When food ran out, as in the winter of 1891–2, millions of people died of starvation.

Source B

I lived near the factory, in a large smelly house, full of poor people. About fifteen of us rented one apartment. I was in a dark, windowless corner room. It was dirty and full of bedbugs and fleas. There was just space for two beds. I shared mine with another man. The rooms stank of the mud from the street, made up of dirt, rubbish and sewage.

▲ S.I. Kanatchikov recalls his life as a factory worker in Moscow in 1900.

Life in the towns

Workers in Russia's main towns (like St. Petersburg) also had a tough life. A normal working day was more than eleven hours, and wages were very low. **Trade unions** were banned and strikes were illegal, so workers could not do much to improve their working conditions. It was hard to find anywhere to live, so many factory workers lived in rooms in houses owned by their employers. These rooms were crammed full of workers, as many as ten to a room, taking it in turns to sleep.

Of course, not all Russians were poor. The nobles were rich and powerful. They owned a quarter of the land and lived a life of luxury, waited on by lots of servants. Some other Russians were rich too – the **capitalists**. They used their money (capital) to set up banks and factories or to trade. The capitalists were able to make huge profits by paying low wages and spending very little to improve working and living conditions for their workers.

Running the country

In 1905, **Tsar Nicholas II** ruled Russia. He was an **autocrat** – he alone ran the country and made the decisions. The Russian people, including peasants and town workers (95% of the population), had no say in the matter. Villages were run by *mirs* (local councils), but they had to obey the government. There was a **Committee of Ministers** to advise the Tsar – but they were nobles that he chose. Newspapers and books were censored (the government controlled what was printed.) The **Okhrana** (state police) watched people against the Tsar. These people usually ended up in exile in bleak and isolated Siberia.

▶ A political cartoon about Russian society, drawn around 1900. The workers at the bottom protest at their lack of freedoms. Next, the capitalists say 'We do the eating'; the army say 'We shoot you'; the clergy say 'We fool you'; and the nobles say 'We govern you'. The royal family at the top say 'We rule you'.

Most people were members of the **Russian Orthodox Church**. Its priests told people it was a sin to oppose the Tsar. The Church owned a lot of land, and the head of the Church was one of the Tsar's ministers.

In 1895, Nicholas' father, **Alexander III**, had called Nicholas 'still absolutely a child, with infantile judgements'. Two years later, he was dead and Nicholas was Tsar. When Nicholas heard that his father was dead, he asked his brother-in-law 'What am I to do? I am not prepared to be Tsar. I know nothing of the business of ruling'. During his reign Nicholas was dominated by his German wife, **Alexandra**, who wanted him to defend his **absolute** (complete) powers against any calls for reform.

1.2 Who opposed the Tsar?

• •

Many Russians believed that God had chosen the Tsar to rule. They believed everyone was born into a particular position in society, and ought to accept this. They should respect and obey the Tsar and nobles. Obviously the Tsar, the nobles and the Church encouraged them to believe this. But not everyone did. Some people looked at the awful lives of the peasants and factory workers and said there had to be changes. Other people saw that countries like Britain and France were run in a more democratic way. People there had a say in how their country was run.

Opposition was illegal, and Nicholas used the Okhrana to arrest and exile thousands of opponents of his rule. However, there were still important opposition groups in Russia.

1 The Liberals

The **Liberals** did not want to overthrow the Tsar. They wanted to keep the Tsar, but wanted him to introduce western democratic ideas. They thought Russia should have an elected parliament (**Duma**). The Liberals were mostly educated, professional people. Their main concern was that Russia should keep up with western countries.

Source **E**

▲ Tsar Nicholas II in 1894.

2 The Social Revolutionary Party

Social Revolutionaries believed that the peasants who farmed the land should own it, not wealthy landowners. They wanted to organize the peasants to revolt against the Tsar. The Social Revolutionaries were prepared to be violent to spark off reforms. Between 1890 and 1905, they killed several members of the government.

3 The Social Democratic Party

Social Democrats also wanted a revolution. They believed in the ideas of a German political thinker, **Karl Marx**. Marx wrote the *Communist Manifesto* in 1848. It set out a plan for revolution. The workers were to take over. Then they had to work to set up a **socialist** system. They would move on from this to a **communist** one (see diagram).

But the Social Democrats disagreed on how to run the revolution. In 1903, the party split into **Mensheviks** and **Bolsheviks**.

The Mensheviks said the revolution would happen when all the workers were ready to take part in it. The Bolsheviks, led by **Lenin**, said the revolution needed to be started and led by a small group of revolutionaries. It was Lenin and the Bolsheviks who were to bring about the communist revolution of November 1917 (see page 28).

THE **MARXIST** VIEW OF HISTORY
from Capitalism to Communism

CAPITALISM

Wealthy people (capitalists), own the land and factories. They employ the workers and keep all the profits that are made.

SOCIALISM

The workers rise up and overthrow their bosses. Now all the land and industry is owned by the government. Strong government is needed to stop the bosses taking over again.

COMMUNISM

Everyone has accepted the new system. There is now a classless system with all working together for the good of everyone.

KARL MARX (1818–33)

Karl Marx was a German thinker who had a great influence on the leaders of the Russian Revolution. He wrote the *Communist Manifesto* (which encouraged workers to take power) and *Das Kapital* (which said everyone should share the wealth of their country). He died in England and is buried in Highgate Cemetery, London.

SUMMARY

Russia in 1905

► The Tsar and nobles were rich and powerful. Most people were poor. The Church and state police supported this system.

► A huge empire, made up of many nationalities, dominated by Russians.

► A growing number of (illegal) groups wanting reforms.

CHAPTER 2

1905: THE YEAR OF CHANGE

2.1 Why was there a revolution in 1905?

By 1905, many Russians wanted to show how they disapproved of the way the Tsar ran the country. The 1905 Revolution broke out. Such violent opposition frightened the Tsar. He agreed to changes, then made sure few of them worked. By 1917 discontent was so great Nicholas was forced to **abdicate** (step down as ruler).

Why did revolution break out in 1905?

First, as we have seen, more and more people were unhappy with the way the country was being run. In 1902, the Minister of the Interior, **Dimitri Sipiagin**, was shot dead by Social Revolutionaries. Nicholas II made **Viacheslev Plehve** the new minister. But Plehve made matters worse. He encouraged attacks on Jews and helped the Okhrana set up fake trade unions (which were illegal) to trap workers. In July 1904, Plehve was assassinated.

The **Russo-Japanese War** in 1905 was the biggest cause of unrest. In 1904, Russia and Japan had begun to fight over control of Manchuria and Korea. The Tsar hoped for a quick victory to make his government more popular. But the war was a disaster. The Russian army suffered a series of defeats. In May 1905, after sailing for seven months from the Baltic Sea, the Russian fleet reached Tsushima. The Japanese sank it the very next day! In September 1905, Russia signed the Treaty of Portsmouth, agreeing to Japanese control of Korea and much of Manchuria.

Source **A**

On 15 October 1904 the Russian Baltic Fleet left its base to relieve the Russian garrison at Port Arthur. It made an extraordinary voyage, only to suffer total defeat.

The Japanese fleet surprised the 27 warships as they steamed through the Straits of Tsushima. The battle was over in ninety minutes. Only three Russian ships made their escape.

▲ B. Catchpole, *A Map History of Russia*, 1974.

▼ The Russo-Japanese War 1904–5.

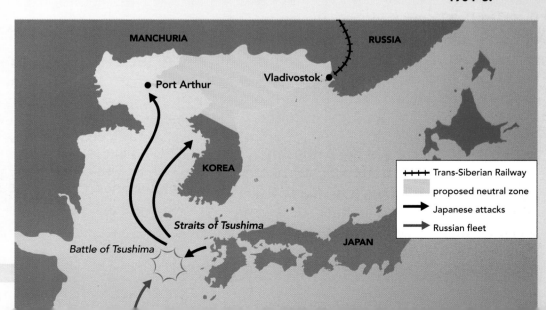

Bloody Sunday

On 22 January 1905, **Father Gapon** led 200,000 workers through the streets of St. Petersburg to the Tsar's **Winter Palace**. They wanted to give him a list of complaints.

Troops, panicked by the size of the crowd, opened fire on the marchers. The government later said 96 people were killed and 333 wounded. The figures were probably much higher. This event became known as **Bloody Sunday**.

Source B

▲ A cartoon from 1905, suggesting revolution was dangerous. The skeleton-like figure is a revolutionary.

2.2 What happened after Bloody Sunday?

1905 – Year of Revolution

Bloody Sunday shocked the world. In Russia there was a wave of protests. Over 500,000 workers went on strike. The Tsar's uncle was assassinated. Nicholas agreed to talk about making reforms.

Russian workers began forming unions to protect their rights. **Industrial** workers set up unions. So did engineers, teachers and lawyers. In May 1905, all these unions joined to form the **Union of Unions**.

In the country, peasants rose up, murdered their landlords and took over the lands. The **minority nationalities** of Russia took this chance to revolt too. These other peoples in the Empire (like the Poles and Armenians) deeply resented being forced by the Tsar to learn Russian and adopt Russian culture.

In June 1905, the crew of the **battleship** *Potemkin* mutinied in support of striking workers. The army moved in. About 2,000 people were killed and another 3,000 were injured before the mutiny was crushed.

In St. Petersburg, the printers went on strike in September 1905. Other trades joined in. The **general strike** which followed crippled the city. Factories, shops and schools closed.

The strikers chose 500 representatives to form a **Soviet** (a council) to organize strikes in the city. Soon Soviets were being elected in towns and cities all over Russia. The Tsar's government was breaking down. It was being replaced by groups elected by the people. These events that followed Bloody Sunday were so serious that they are usually called the **1905 Revolution**.

GEORGY GAPON (1870–1906)

Father Gapon was the priest who led the marchers on Bloody Sunday. He may have been a police informer. After Bloody Sunday he left Russia. When he returned, in 1906, he was captured by the Social Revolutionaries. They hanged him as a police spy.

10 CHAPTER 2 1905: THE YEAR OF CHANGE

The October Manifesto

Nicholas II survived the 1905 Revolution. Much of the credit for this lies with **Sergei Witte**, his Chief Minister. He persuaded the Tsar to make **concessions**. By giving in to some of the demands for change the Tsar hoped to win the support of the Liberals and ignore the more extreme demands of the revolutionaries. On 17 October 1905, Nicholas issued the October Manifesto. It set out political rights for the people of Russia. It set up a voting system for an elected parliament – a **Duma**.

Revenge

As the Tsar regained control, his supporters came back out into the open. Landowners, government officials and churchmen loyal to the Tsar now formed organizations called Black Hundreds, and murdered thousands of the Tsar's opponents. The police and army stood by and let it happen.

A Duma was to be elected in Russia.

All Russian men had the right to vote.

All laws made in Russia had to be approved by the Duma.

The Russian people were to have the right to form political parties, have freedom of speech and hold meetings as they liked.

Source C

The October Manifesto was greeted with delight. The **St. Petersburg Soviet** called off the general strike and strikers in other cities also went back to work. Some revolutionaries warned that Nicholas could not be trusted and that any opposition would be punished.

They were right. Leaders of the St. Petersburg Soviet were arrested and exiled. When the **Moscow Soviet** organized an uprising at the end of 1905, the army crushed it in a battle which cost over a thousand lives. Peasants who had burned their landlords' farms were hanged and the Tsar's authority was restored throughout the Russian Empire.

▲ A modern historian commenting on how the Tsar soon restored his control after the October Manifesto was published.

WITTE (1845-1915)

Sergei Witte was the first Russian prime minister. Although he attempted to give the Tzar good advice, it was rarely taken.

◄ Concessions made by the Tsar in the October Manifesto. He was afraid he would be assassinated if he did not make them.

The Dumas

In the October Manifesto of 1905, the Tsar promised political rights and a Duma to help run the country. But Nicholas believed in his right to absolute power. It was unlikely that he would allow any interference.

In March 1906, elections for the first Duma were held. The voting system worked against the peasants and workers. Even so, most of those elected were critical of the government. But Nicholas made sure the Duma had no real power. In May, he issued the **Fundamental Laws**. These gave him total control over the Duma. He alone could make laws. He could **dissolve** (dismiss) the Duma, or change the way it was elected, any time he liked.

- The first Duma met in May 1906. It tried to appoint ministers and to have more say in running the country. So Nicholas sent his troops to dissolve it. Russia's first parliament had lasted just over two months.
- A second Duma, elected in 1907, lasted five months. Then Nicholas dissolved it for criticizing his government. He then changed the voting system.
- In the third Duma the richest 1% of Russians elected two-thirds of the representatives. Not suprisingly, Nicholas had little trouble from this Duma. It lasted the full five years that it was allowed to run.
- The fourth Duma, elected in 1912, also obeyed him.

Repression and reform

In 1906, the Social Revolutionaries began a terrorist campaign to show that the Tsar's government had lost control. Thousands of Russians were killed or injured. The Tsar dismissed Witte. He blamed Witte for the October Manifesto, which had not kept the Tsar's opponents quiet after all.

Nicholas then appointed **Peter Stolypin** as Chief Minister. Stolypin promised that he would bring 'repression and reform'.

Source D

The Tsar alone makes laws.

The Tsar alone controls foreign affairs.

The Tsar alone decides military matters.

Ministers are appointed and dismissed by the Tsar alone.

The Tsar may dissolve the Duma when he chooses.

The system for electing the Duma is the responsibility of the Tsar alone.

▲ **Some of the Fundamental Laws issued by Nicholas II in 1906.**

Source E

We talked for two hours. He shook my hand. He wished me all the luck in the world. I went home happy, only to find a written order dismissing me lying on my desk.

▲ **Sergei Witte describes his dismissal in 1906.**

SUMMARY

▶ **1905** Tsar made concessions in the October Manifesto.
Black Hundreds attacked Tsar's opponents.

▶ **1906** First Duma met and was dissolved.
Tsar changed system of voting.
Stolypin introduced 'repression and reform'.
Revolutionary activity died down.

Stolypin and repression

Stolypin set up special courts called 'Field Courts for Civilians'. These held quick trials for those who were 'obviously guilty'. The accused were always found guilty. They had no right to appeal against the sentence of exile or execution. By the end of 1906, over 1,000 'terrorists' had been tried and executed. A further 20,000 revolutionaries had been exiled to Siberia. Russians started to call the hangman's rope 'Stolypin's necktie'. Estimated numbers of revolutionaries in Russia fell from 100,000 in 1905 to 10,000 in 1910.

Stolypin and reform

Stolypin also introduced reforms to help the peasants. He hoped that better living conditions would make them less likely to support the revolutionary groups.

Stolypin lent peasants money to help them to buy land from their local village commune (*mir*). *Mirs* had owned the land since peasants were freed from **serfdom** in 1861. By 1914, over 2,000,000 peasants owned their land. But only the richest could buy enough land to grow enough to support their families. Most peasants still struggled to make ends meet. Russian farming methods were very inefficent, compared to those in other western countries.

Stolypin's tough measures meant there was less trouble in the factories and mines. So there were fewer strikes. In the period immediately after 1905, Russia's industrial production rose. But in 1912, strikes broke out again and industrial production fell (see diagram).

▼ Russian industrial production 1900–14.

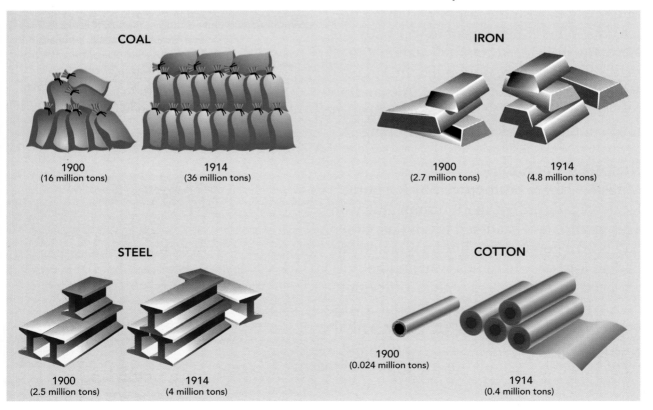

COAL
1900
(16 million tons)
1914
(36 million tons)

IRON
1900
(2.7 million tons)
1914
(4.8 million tons)

STEEL
1900
(2.5 million tons)
1914
(4 million tons)

COTTON
1900
(0.024 million tons)
1914
(0.4 million tons)

Stolypin had settled Russia, and the Tsar was again in control. But in September 1911, Stolypin was assassinated. He had been finding it harder and harder to get the Tsar to take his advice anyway. The Tsar was falling under the spell of **Grigory Rasputin**.

Who was Rasputin?

Rasputin was a peasant who saw himself as a holy man. He came to the royal court in 1905. Nicholas's son, **Alexei**, had a rare illness called **haemophilia**. His blood did not clot. Even a small cut or bruise might cause him to bleed to death. Doctors could not cure this, but Rasputin could calm Alexei. It was said he had even managed to stop internal bleeding. The royal family, especially the Tsarina, Alexandra, began to see Rasputin as vital to Alexei's health.

Rasputin and Alexandra

Alexandra was a German. She was already unpopular in Russia for insisting Nicholas must cling to absolute power and make no reforms. When Russia went to war with Germany in 1914, Alexandra's nationality made her even more unpopular. In August 1915, the Tsar went to the Front. Alexandra was left in charge in St. Petersburg. She turned to Rasputin for advice about everything.

Rasputin in charge

Ministers had to be approved by Rasputin. He even gave orders about running the war. This would have mattered less if Rasputin had been a good leader. But he was not. He had no idea how to fight a war, and he replaced good ministers with incompetent ones who flattered him. Soon Rasputin was being blamed for all that was wrong with the Tsar's government. Many of the problems were not really his fault (for instance, the food shortages in the towns caused by the war).

Source F

▲ A Russian cartoon, published in 1916, showing Rasputin with the Tsar and Tsarina in each hand. The cartoonist is trying to show the power Rasputin had over them.

Source G

You must be my eyes and ears there in the capital, while I stay here. It is up to you to keep peace among the ministers. Do this and you do a great service to me and our country.

▲ Part of a letter written by the Tsar to his wife in 1915 from the Front.

Hatred of Rasputin

Things got rapidly worse. Rasputin had so much power over the Tsarina that she did not listen to anyone else. The nobles resented him because they lost power and had to be polite to him, a peasant. They thought his behaviour was appalling. He was loud, rude and had no manners. He had affairs with scores of women and did not keep them secret.

Assassination!

Alexandra ignored all this, saying: 'guided by him we will get through this heavy time'. It was clear that she would never send Rasputin away. In desperation a group of nobles assassinated Rasputin in December 1916.

But the damage was done. The Tsar, it was said, was not fit to rule. He had allowed his German wife and a crazy monk to run the country while he went to fight the war. More and more Russians came to believe that the Tsar had to go.

Source H

There was nothing the Tsarina would not do for those she loved. She was sure Rasputin was God's chosen one (had she not seen God answer his prayers when her son was ill?). She was sure he could use his powers to keep the Tsar in power and to keep her son alive. Without him her family was lost.

▲ Peter Gilliard, who was the private teacher of Nicholas and Alexandra's son Alexei, talking about the hold Rasputin had over the royal family.

Source I

Now I must give you a message from our friend [Rasputin], prompted by what he saw in his dreams last night. He begs you to advance near Riga. He says it is necessary, otherwise the Germans will settle down so firmly for the winter that it will cost endless lives and trouble to make them move.

▲ Part of a letter from the Tsarina to the Tsar in 1915.

▼Rasputin after his murder in 1916.

Source J

ALEXANDRA (1872–1918?)

Tsarina Alexandra was a German princess who married Nicholas in 1892. She was a strong supporter of his absolute rule. When Nicholas went to fight in the war, Alexandra followed the advice of Gregori Rasputin. This made the Tsar's rule even more unpopular. Alexandra, her husband and most of her family were probably shot in the Ipatiev House in 1918.

Source 1

▲ A photograph of Bloody Sunday.

Source 2

Sire

We workers and inhabitants of St. Petersburg come to you to seek truth and defence.

We have been oppressed. We are seen not as human beings, but as slaves who must endure their bitter fate in silence.

We asked our masters to discuss our needs with us, but they refused, saying we have no right to make such a request.

We asked that the working day be reduced to eight hours, that the minumum daily wage be made one rouble, that overtime be abolished. We asked that medical attention be provided and that workshop conditions be improved. It is almost impossible to work in these places and not fall ill and die from awful draughts, rain and snow.

All these requests our employers described as illegal. Every one was called a crime. Our desire to improve our condition was regarded as impertinent and offensive.

▲ Extracts from the petition taken to the Winter Palace on Bloody Sunday.

Source 3

▲ A French picture drawn shortly after Bloody Sunday.

Source 4

▲ A German cartoon of 1905, claiming to show the events of Bloody Sunday.

Source 5

22 January 1905
Disorders in St. Petersburg because workers wanted to come to the Winter Palace. Troops had to open fire in several places. There were many killed and wounded. God, how painful and sad! Mama arrived, straight to Mass. I lunched with all the others. Went for a walk, with Misha. Mama stayed overnight.

▲ Extract from the diary of Tsar Nicholas II.

Source 6

The marchers sang hymns and 'God Save the Tsar'. They carried religious pictures and ones of the Tsar. Long before they reached Palace Square, the separate groups of marchers were met by Cossacks [soldiers on horses] and foot soldiers.

They were ordered to go home. When they did not, soldiers fired into the defenceless crowd of men, women and children. Within minutes hundreds were dead and many more injured.

▲ From David Floyd, 'Russia 1905–12', History of the Twentieth Century.

What happened on Bloody Sunday?

One of the most exciting activities in the study of history is working out what happened using sources from the time. These very seldom give exactly the same view of an event.

This is true of sources about Bloody Sunday. Source 6 suggests there was a violent attack on peaceful marchers. The two foreign pictures (Sources 3 and 4) support this. But the image of peaceful innocence is not supported as clearly by Source 1. Historians would want to consider just how reliable the two drawings are. They would also want to consider if the photo is typical of everything that was going on.

CHAPTER 3

THE IMPACT OF THE FIRST WORLD WAR

Source A

In August 1914, Russia joined Britain and France fighting against Austria-Hungary, Germany and (from October) Turkey. At first, Russians supported the war. Anti-German feeling was so great that Nicholas re-named the capital Petrograd (St. Petersburg sounded too German).

Success and failure

In the first weeks of the war, the Russians moved rapidly into German territory. But then they stopped winning. The Germans moved troops from the Western Front eastwards. Within weeks they had won two huge victories over the Russians. At the battle of **Tannenberg** they trapped Russian troops in swampland. About 90,000 Russians were captured and over 100,000 drowned. A week later the Germans slaughtered a further 100,000 Russians at the battle of **Masurian Lakes**.

▲ A Russian First World War poster. The might of Russia (the medieval Russian knight) attacks a three headed monster. One head (Austria) is cut off. Another head (Germany) has been wounded.

The Tsar takes command

By the end of 1914, the Russian army had lost over a million men. In the spring of 1915, German troops advanced over 450 km into Russia. Nicholas took over command of the army. But this was a mistake. He was now held directly to blame for the slaughter. In early 1916, Nicholas ordered an attack on Germany which failed, with heavy Russian casualties. In June 1916 a Russian advance into Austria failed again. Over a million more Russians died. Another million soldiers deserted and went home.

The Russian people blamed the Tsar for leaving his wife and Rasputin to run the country. Success in the war might have helped him set things straight. Failure was a disaster.

Source B

It was a ghastly sight. Thousands of men, with their guns, horses and ammunition, struggled in the water of the two huge swamps. To shorten their agony, our men turned their machine guns on them.

▲ The German general, von Moltke, describes how the Germans slaughtered the Russian troops at Tannenberg.

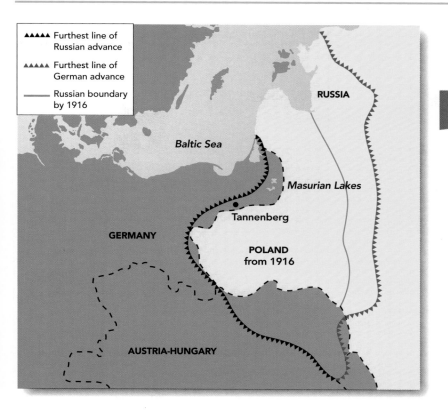

Legend:
- ▲▲▲▲▲ Furthest line of Russian advance
- ▲▲▲▲▲ Furthest line of German advance
- —— Russian boundary by 1916

RUSSIA

Baltic Sea

Masurian Lakes

Tannenberg

GERMANY

POLAND from 1916

AUSTRIA-HUNGARY

Source C

Processions in the streets carried the Tsar's portrait, framed in the flags of the Allies [Britain and France]. Bands played the national anthem. A long line of khaki-clad figures marched away, singing and cheering.

They were tall men with honest, open faces, and a trusting faith in the Tsar – certain that the saints would protect them and bring them safely back.

▲ Meriel Buchanan, whose father was the British Ambassador in St. Petersburg from 1910 to 1918. She is describing the Russian army leaving for war, August 1914.

The collapse of the Russian economy

The war ruined the Russian economy. **Inflation** meant that by 1917, things cost about seven times as much as in 1913. Huge numbers of men went to war, leaving too few to grow the food that Russia needed. Horses were also taken to the Front. This made farming even harder.

Industry had fewer workers, too. As the war dragged on, fuel and other supplies ran out. The transport system could not move soldiers, food supplies and supplies for factories at the same time. The war came first.

Source D

	1914	1915	1916	1917
Men mobilized (millions)	6.5	11.2	14.2	15.1
% of working males in army	14.9	25.9	35.7	36.7
Grain production (in poods)*	3509	4006	3319	3185
Inflation (taking a 1913 rouble as 100)	130	155	300	755

* 1 pood = 18kg

◄ The economic effect of the First World War on Russia.

As more men went to war, fewer worked on the land producing food. Prices shot up.

3.1 Why did Russia do so badly in the War?

Source 1

The soldiers accuse the military authorities of corruption, cowardice, drunkenness, and even treason.

Deserters are everywhere, committing crimes and threatening civilians. The civilians say they regret the Germans did not invade, take over and restore order.

▲ A Petrograd police report of army morale in October 1916.

Source 2

If we have three days of serious fighting we might run out of ammunition altogether. Without new rifles we cannot fill the gaps.

The army is now almost stronger than in peace time; it should be [and it was at the beginning] three times as strong.

▲ Part of a letter from the Tsar to the Tsarina, written in July 1915.

Source 3

The workers are not in a patriotic mood. The high cost of living, overwork, and barbaric government policies have shown the masses the true nature of the war.

There are more and more strikes all over the country. Prices have gone up five to ten times in the last year. Clothes and shoes are hard to get. It is impossible to get meat.

▲ A letter written by a revolutionary to Lenin, the leader of the Bolsheviks, in December 1916.

Source 4

Despite all the losses, at the start of 1917 Russia looked strong enough to fight on. The war economy was going full-blast.

The Russian generals were confident. They had more men, more guns, and more ammunition than the enemy.

▲ Tony Howarth, *Twentieth Century History: the World Since 1900*, Longman, 1979.

▼ *'Everything for the War'*. A Russian poster encouraging women to work in munitions factories.

Source 5

Source 6

◄ Russian prisoners of war under guard in May 1915.

Source 7

Things are getting worse. The men are splendid, there are plenty of guns and ammunition. But the strategies of the generals are brainless. We are ready to die for Russia, but not for the whim of a general.

▲ Extract from a letter home by an officer in the army in late 1916.

Source 8

▲ An anti-war poster issued by the Bolsheviks during the war. It shows the Tsar, the Church and the Russian nobility riding on the shoulders of ordinary Russians.

Russia and the First World War

Some historians believe that Russia's defeat in the First World War was the main cause of the Tsar's fall from power. Many people were killed and the war led to serious shortages and discontent all over Russia.

The lack of support for the Tsar is highlighted in Source 1. Some Russian civilians would have chosen German rule, as more likely to provide law and order than the rule of the Tsar. Sources 2 and 3 emphasize the problems created by the war.

The theory that Russia was defeated by shortages is challenged by Sources 4 and 7. They suggest that leadership was lacking, not supplies. Source 8 shows how the Tsar's political opponents used the war as an opportunity to attack his government.

CHAPTER 4

1917: THE YEAR OF REVOLUTIONS

In January 1917, the Tsar still ruled Russia. Inefficiency, corruption and losses in the war had made his rule very unpopular. Even so, few people can have expected that he would soon be forced to **abdicate** (stop ruling) by the **March Revolution**. Even fewer would have thought that the **Provisional Government** that took over from the Tsar would also be swept from power by revolution. From November 1917, Russia was governed by the **Bolsheviks** – people who just a few months earlier had been living in exile, forced out by the Tsar's government.

In 1918 the Bolshevik government changed the Russian calendar. Before this, Russian dates had been two weeks ahead of Europe. So the revolutions which were in March and November in Russia were in February and October in the rest of Europe. All dates in this book are based on the **Russian calendar.**

4.1 Why did the Tsar abdicate in March 1917?

The overthrow of the Tsar happened more by chance than by any great plan. Some historians even argue that the March Revolution was sparked off by the weather. The first months of 1917 were much colder than usual – temperatures averaged –12°C. This extreme cold, on top of food and fuel shortages due to the war, was too much.

First steps to revolution

The revolution began in the capital, Petrograd. Women who had queued for hours were told there was no bread in the shops. So they attacked the bakeries. Next day thousands of workers began protest strikes. Crowds gathered, shouting anti-government slogans.

On 9 March, a crowd of 200,000 gathered in the city centre. Revolutionaries gave out leaflets calling for the overthrow of the government. Shops were raided and buildings were set on fire. The Tsar ordered **General Khabolov** (commander of the city's troops) to stop the 'disorders' which he said were 'unacceptable'. But Khabolov's troops were new recruits. Many of them sympathized with the rioters – they too were hungry.

Source A

The strikers and rioters in the city are now angrier than ever. The trouble comes from idle people, wounded soldiers, school girls and people like that. They run around saying they have no bread, just to create some excitement.

But things will settle down. They say it is different from 1905 as they all worship you and only want bread.

▲ Letter from the Tsarina Alexandra to Nicholas, 10 March 1917.

On 11 March, things reached boiling point. Some of Khabolov's troops fired on rioting strikers. Some refused to do so. The Duma sent frantic messages to Nicholas at the Front. They said he needed to form a government which the people would support. But Nicholas did not understand the seriousness of the situation. He dissolved the Duma saying, 'That fat **Rodzyanko** (see Source B) has sent me some nonsense to which I will not even reply'.

By the end of the next day, the capital was out of control. Troops refused to shoot strikers. One regiment killed its officers and joined the demonstrators. Others followed them. Many handed over their weapons to the strikers. Petrograd's garrison fell from 34,000 to less than 2,000. The city was in the hands of revolutionaries.

Abdication

The Tsar saw how bad the situation was too late. He tried to return to Petrograd, but his train was stopped at Pskov. It was not safe to go further. On 15 March, Nicholas **abdicated**. His brother, the Grand Duke Michael, refused to become Tsar. The monarchy in Russia was finished.

▼ Soldiers joining the revolution in Petrograd in March 1918.

Source B

Petrograd is in a state of **anarchy** [out of control]. The government is paralysed; the transport system is broken down; the food and fuel supplies are disorganized. Discontent is rising. There is shooting on the streets; troops are firing at each other.

▲ Telegram sent by Rodzyanko, President of the Duma, to the Tsar on 11 March 1917.

RODZYANKO (1859–1924)

Michael Rodzyanko, president of the Duma, helped set up the Provisional Government. He opposed the Bolshevik takeover and fled Russia in 1920.

Source C

4.2 What did the Provisional Government achieve?

The Duma met on 11 March, despite orders from the Tsar to break up. Russia was in the middle of a revolution. But who would win? Should the Duma obey the Tsar or use the revolution to take power? They decided to form a 'Provisional Government' until a new Duma could be elected. The Provisional Government held a mix of political views. The new Prime Minister, **Prince Lvov**, was a noble. Most of the other members were Liberals. But **Alexander Kerensky**, the Minister of Justice, was an important Social Revolutionary.

The Petrograd Soviet

During March 1917, workers in Petrograd had formed a Soviet (workers' council) like the one set up in the 1905 Revolution. The Soviet had 3,000 members. Each of them represented up to 1,000 workers or soldiers. The Soviet ran Petrograd, and the Provisional Government could not rule without its support. Kerensky (a leading Soviet member) was in the government to give the Soviet a voice. In the early months of its life, the Provisional Government had the support of the Petrograd Soviet, but that support was short-lived.

The war drags on

The Provisional Government decided to continue the war. Many of its members felt the war could be won. If they won the war people would support them. But they were no more successful at war than the Tsar had been. A new attack in the summer of 1917 was a terrible failure. There were strikes and rioting in the streets. At the Front, soldiers deserted in their thousands. The longer the war dragged on, the more unpopular the new

Source D

It inherited nothing from the Tsar, but a terrible war, a shortage of food, a paralysed transport system, no money, and a population in a state of furious discontent.

▲ Alexander Kerensky commenting on the Provisional Goverment's position in 1917.

Source E

1   In all military groups, and on naval vessels, committees from elected representatives of the lower ranks shall be chosen at once.

2   Orders of the Duma will be carried out only when they do not go against the orders of the Soviet of Workers' and Soldiers' Deputies.

6   Standing to attention and saluting when not on duty is abolished.

7   Addressing of the officers as 'Your Excellency' etc is abolished. These titles are replaced by 'Mister General' etc.

▲ Extracts from 'Military Order No. 1' issued by the Petrograd Soviet on 27 March 1917.

SUMMARY

▶ **9 March**
Anti-government riots in Petrograd.

▶ **11 March**
Troops opened fire on demonstrators.
Duma dissolved.

▶ **12 March**
Government lost control in Petrograd.
Troops deserted.

▶ **15 March**
Tsar Nicholas abdicated.
Provisional Government set up.

High hopes

The Provisional Government also had to deal with the high hopes created by the overthrow of the Tsar. The peasants expected land to be taken from the nobles and shared out. But this would have been impossible because the Provisional Government did not control enough of Russia. Even if it had, not many of its members wanted such extreme changes. They agreed to delay most decisions until elections in November. This frustrated many Russians who wanted much quicker reform.

The wrong reforms?

The government did make some changes. Political prisoners were freed. Freedom of speech and of the press were introduced. But unfortunately for the government, this meant that its opponents could now make their voices heard more easily.

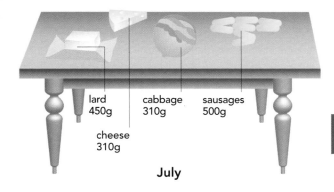

lard
450g

cabbage
310g

sausages
500g

cheese
310g

July

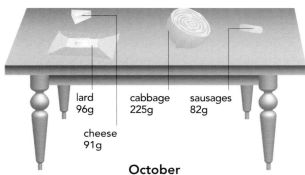

lard
96g

cabbage
225g

sausages
82g

cheese
91g

October

▲ Inflation in 1917. What a rouble could buy in July and October.

▲ A poster issued by the Provisional Government trying to raise enthusiasm for continuing the war. It shows a Russian soldier backed by workers and soldiers.

Source G

With no guns it is hard to keep order. The new government does not give us any support. We only have two soldiers to keep order in fifty villages. We should have at least fifty armed men, telephones, cars.

Young hooligans steal horses and cattle and run riot. We can do nothing. We can't even call for help if they set a house or village on fire. They broke into Prince C's house, stole all his papers and wrecked the place.

▲ Said to Ernest Poole, an American visitor, by the head of the local unit of soldiers in a small village near Petrograd.

The revolutionaries come back

Among the government's political enemies were revolutionaries exiled during the Tsar's reign. When the Tsar abdicated they returned to Russia, making further problems for the government.

Lenin's return

One such revolutionary was **Lenin**, leader of the Bolsheviks (see pages 8 and 29). The Germans supported the Bolsheviks, and laid on a train for Lenin to return to Russia, hoping he could get the government to pull out of the war. But Lenin had been away too long. He found the Bolsheviks had little influence in the government. Lenin's political ideas also had little support, even in his own party. First, he needed to get other Bolsheviks to agree with his ideas.

The Bolsheviks gain support

During 1917, Lenin and his supporters steadily spread their views. Bolsheviks who were won over made speeches in factories and at the Front. They delivered Lenin's ideas, simplified into the slogan **Peace, Land and Bread**. The Bolshevik newspaper *Pravda* (Truth) poured out anti-government propaganda As a result, support for the Bolsheviks grew rapidly.

▲ A painting of Lenin addressing the crowd at Finland Station on his return to Russia in April 1917.

Source **H**

1 From 1 to 7 April, 7,688 men deserted.

3 Officers and commanders have lost control.

5 Anti-war pamphlets and propaganda are everywhere in the army.

▲ Parts of a report made by the War Minister, Alexander Guchkov, to the Provisional Government in April 1917.

KERENSKY (1881–1970)

Alexander Kerensky was born in Simbursk. Lenin was also born there and was taught at school by Kerensky's father.

Kerensky studied law at St. Petersburg University. He joined the Social Revolutionaries in 1905. He was elected to the Duma in 1912 and in 1917 was made President of the Provisional Government. After the November Revolution, Kerensky tried to organize resistance to the Bolsheviks. He failed. He fled abroad to France and finally settled in the USA.

The July Days riots

The Provisional Government became more and more unpopular. 500,000 workers went on strike in Petrograd. Soldiers, sailors and workers rioted in the city. They called for an end to the war and demanded a Bolshevik government. This rising became known as the **July Days**. The Bolsheviks had not planned this. Lenin believed they were not yet ready to take over. Kerensky (who had become Prime Minister in July) acted swiftly. He arrested hundreds of Bolsheviks and accused Lenin of being a German agent. Lenin was forced to flee to Finland.

Struggle for power

Kerensky made **General Kornilov** Supreme Commander of the Russian army. Kornilov wanted to bring back the death penalty for people who opposed the government. He thought Kerensky was not being hard enough. In September, he tried take over and use the army to run Russia as a **military dictatorship**. Kerensky had to release the arrested Bolsheviks to help fight Kornilov. This worked. Kornilov did not have enough support and was arrested by Kerensky's men.

4.3 How did the Bolsheviks seize power?

By the autumn of 1917, the Provisional Government faced huge difficulties. The war was going badly. People had to cope with inflation and food shortages. Most Russians were unhappy about the slow pace of reform, and the Bolsheviks were working to overthrow the government. But, in the end, events moved faster than the Bolsheviks planned.

Source J

We sent sailors to the telephone exchange, to place two small guns at the entrance. The telephone girls fled with hysterical screams. The sailors managed to run the switchboard themselves. So we began to take over the administration.

At the railway terminals, our Commissaries watch the incoming and outgoing trains.

▲ Trotsky describes the events of 7 November 1917.

Source K

◀ The Women's Death Battalion. They defended the Winter Palace on 7–8 November.

Ready for action

The Bolsheviks were given weapons to fight Kornilov, but they kept them. They already controlled the Petrograd and Moscow Soviets. Lenin saw that, while he really wanted longer to prepare for revolution, the time had come to act. In October 1917, he returned to Petrograd. He and Trotsky planned to launch the revolution on 7 November, when all the Soviets of Russia met in the capital.

The Bolsheviks make their move

On 7 November, the Bolsheviks seized control of strategic points in the city. The next morning, Lenin told the press that the Provisional Government had been deposed. It was ordered to surrender or be attacked by the *Aurora* (a ship which the Bolsheviks had moored opposite the Winter Palace). There was some resistance, but the government soon surrendered and the Bolsheviks took over the Winter Palace. There had been just five deaths. Prime Minister Kerensky escaped from Petrograd. He asked troops at the Front to return to Petrograd to fight the Bolsheviks, but the troops refused. The Bolsheviks were now running the country.

▲ Extracts from posters announcing the Bolshevik revolution to the people of Petrograd, 8 November 1917.

Map of Petrograd showing the events of 7–8 November.

SAMOILOVA (1876–1921)

The Bolsheviks saw women more as equals. Konkordiya Samoilova set up the paper *Woman Worker* in 1913.

◀ The events of 7–8 November.

① **Early morning 7 November:** Red Guard take main bridges, P.O. and telegraph office

② **Day of 7 November:** railway stations taken, more bridges, electrical station and bank

③ **7–8 November:** St Peter and St Paul Fortress, Winter Palace taken

Vladimir Ulyanov
LENIN

Vladimir Ulyanov was born in Simbirsk, on the river Volga, in 1870. His parents were teachers. In 1887, Lenin's brother, Alexander, was executed for taking part in a plot to blow up Alexander III. Lenin is said to have been against the monarchy from this point.

In 1887, Lenin went to Kazan University to study law. He was expelled for revolutionary activity. He went to St. Petersburg University in 1890 and graduated top of his year in law. He read books by Karl Marx, smuggling some into Russia after a visit to Europe in 1895. He was exiled to Siberia in 1897. He spent most of the years 1900–17 in exile. He returned to Russia in April 1917, after the March Revolution.

Joseph Djugashvili
STALIN

Stalin was born in 1879, in Georgia, Russia. His father was a bootmaker. His mother worked hard to pay for his education. Stalin worked well at school, but was expelled from college in 1899 for not taking his exams. He was more interested in studying the ideas of Karl Marx and working for the revolution.

Stalin was prepared to break the law in support of his ideas. Between 1905 and 1908, he took part in over 1,000 raids to seize money for Bolshevik funds.

Stalin spent much of the period 1905–17 either in exile in Siberia or on the run from the authorities in Russia. He was freed from exile in Siberia in 1917 and returned to Petrograd. He became editor of *Pravda*, the Bolshevik newspaper.

Lev Bronstein
TROTSKY

Trotsky was born in 1879 in the southern Ukraine. He was the son of a Jewish farmer and was educated at Odessa University. At university he read books by Karl Marx. He wrote pamphlets and articles supporting revolutionary ideas. His opposition to the government meant that he spent long periods in exile, both in Siberia and abroad.

Unlike Stalin and Lenin, Trotsky first joined the Mensheviks (see page 8). He joined the Bolsheviks in 1917. Trotsky returned to Petrograd from exile in May 1917 and played a major part in organizing the Bolshevik takeover in November.

1 The problem

After the Bolsheviks took power, a civil war broke out between their supporters (the Reds) and those against Bolshevism (the Whites). Some Whites wanted the Tsar back. The Bolsheviks captured the Russian royal family, the Romanovs, to prevent this. They took them to Ekaterinburg in the Ural mountains on 30 April 1918. The Romanovs were last seen alive on 16 July 1918.

The Romanovs' disappearance probably means they were killed. There were two investigations into their disappearance (in 1918 and 1919). Both were headed by judges who supported the Whites.

2 The evidence from the time

Source 1

Ekaterinburg was threatened by an advance of White gangs, hoping to snatch out of our hands the crowned hangman [the Tsar].

We, the leaders of the Ural Soviet, decided to execute, by shooting, Nicholas Romanov. This was done on 16 July. The wife and son of Romanov have been sent to a secure place.

▲ Statement published in 1918, by Bolsheviks in Moscow.

Source 2

All were dead except for Alexei. Before my eyes Yurosky shot him two or three times and he stopped moaning. I saw these people dead: Nicholas, Alexandra, Alexei, his four daughters, Dr. Botkin, his cook, assistant and maid.

▲ Part of the testimony of Pavel Medevedev, a guard at Ipatiev House, Ekaterinburg. It was given to Judge Sokolov (who led the 1919 investigation).

POINTS TO CONSIDER

1 Both investigations at the time were made by opponents of the Bolsheviks.

2 If other countries knew the Bolsheviks had executed the Romanovs, they might send troops to help the Whites.

3 If the Tsar was dead, some Whites might see little point in continuing to fight.

4 Ekaterinburg was held by the Reds on 16 July 1918. White forces were closing in. They captured the town on 25 July.

5 During the Civil War, officers on both sides sometimes had to make decisions without contacting headquarters.

6 From 1918 to 1987, the government of Russia never discussed the Romanovs. Most Russians thought they were exiled.

Source 3

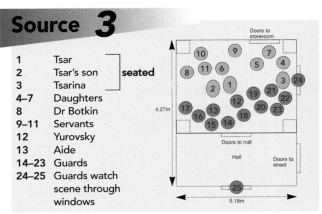

1	Tsar	
2	Tsar's son	seated
3	Tsarina	
4–7	Daughters	
8	Dr Botkin	
9–11	Servants	
12	Yurovsky	
13	Aide	
14–23	Guards	
24–25	Guards watch scene through windows	

▲ A diagram from Judge Sokolov's report showing the position of people in the room.

Source 4

The corpses of the seven Romanovs and their servants were taken to Four Brother's mine at night. The bodies were chopped up, destroyed with sulphuric acid, and burnt.

▲ Part of the report by Judge Sokolov in 1919.

Source 5

Sergeyev said 'I have all the evidence in the Romanov case. I do not believe everyone was shot in the Ipatiev House. The Tsarina, the Tsar's son, and four other children were not shot there. The Tsar, his doctor, two servants and the maid were.'

▲ An interview with Sergeyev (judge in the 1918 investigation) printed in the *New York Tribune* in December 1918.

3 The recent evidence

Since 1918, various people have claimed to be one of the Romanov children who escaped. Because we do not know what happened, these claims have been hard to judge. One of the most widely accepted claims was made in 1922 by a women called Anna Anderson. She said she was Anastasia and that she had hidden behind her sisters during the shooting. When it was all over, a kind Bolshevik soldier took pity on her and rescued her.

In 1991, bones were found in a forest near Ekaterinburg. They were brought to Britain, where advances in forensic science (especially DNA sampling) meant tests could virtually prove whose bones they were.

Source 6

DNA tests identify Tsar's skeleton

British scientists have proved almost beyond doubt that bones unearthed in Russia in 1991 are those of Tsar Nicholas II and his family. They say there is a 98.5% probability that the bones are Romanov. Two members of the royal family remain unaccounted for; the Tsar's heir, Alexei, and one of his daughters.

▲ Account from *The Times*, 10 July 1993.

▼ Photographs of Nicholas and Alexandra, together with the bones found at Ekaterinburg. From *The Times*, 18 September 1993.

What happened to the Romanovs?

The information and sources on these pages show that it is far from clear what happened to the Romanovs. Everyone had an interest in giving their own version of the truth.

The further we are away from events the harder it can be to find evidence, to find witnesses who can still remember what went on. Even the evidence of the latest DNA testing is not completely conclusive and does not account for the bodies of the Tsar's son and one of his daughters. We may never find out exactly what happened.

Source 7

CHAPTER 5

LENIN AND THE ESTABLISHMENT OF THE USSR

In November 1917, the Bolsheviks seized power in Petrograd. They had two tasks. First, they had to take control of all of Russia, not just the capital. Second, they had to hold on to power. The Bolsheviks knew that they had to act faster than the Provisional Government had. They had to get out of the First World War and introduce reforms quickly.

But first they had to fight a civil war to beat their enemies (the Whites). Other countries that were against the Bolsheviks sent help to the Whites. The Bolsheviks won, but the harsh measures they had to use lost them many supporters. They could only keep power if they watered down their communist policies.

5.1 What problems did the Bolsheviks face in November 1917?

The Bolsheviks had taken power in November 1917 with very little bloodshed. But the revolution had broken out too soon – the Army, the Soviets, the Party were not ready. The Bolsheviks ran Petrograd. But would the rest of the country accept them? One week after taking power, the Bolsheviks captured Moscow. Lenin's government sent telegrams all over Russia explaining what had happened in Petrograd. Some areas, like Finland, declared independence from Russia. Most major towns and cities elected Soviets. But in some areas, people resisted the Bolsheviks. It took a three-year civil war for the Bolsheviks to win control of the whole country.

Lenin set up a temporary government, the **Sovnarkom**, or Council of People's **Commissars** (loyal party members). Most of its members were Bolsheviks, but Lenin also chose some Mensheviks and Social Revolutionaries to gain their support. The Sovnarkom discussed policies, but Lenin and his advisers made the decisions. Bolshevik rule was by **decrees** (orders) issued by Prime Minister Lenin.

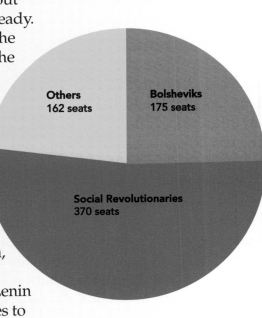

▲ The share of seats in the Constituent Assembly after the elections of November 1917.

An elected government?

Lenin allowed the election arranged by the Provisional Government for November 1917 to take place. The result was an overwhelming victory for his political rivals, the Social Revolutionaries (see page 8). So, when the Assembly met for the first time on 18 January 1918, Lenin sent troops to dissolve it.

Keeping their promises

Lenin now had to keep the promises that he had made. The Bolshevik slogan of 'Peace, Land and Bread' had been highly popular. Lenin had seen the Provisional Government fail by not getting Russia out of the war and not improving the lives of the poor quickly enough. His government had to avoid making the same mistakes.

5.2 How did Lenin keep the Bolsheviks in power?

Although his government effectively controlled only a small part of Russia, Lenin immediately made reforms. He also changed the name of the Bolshevik Party to the **Communist Party**. In 1918, he decreed that the only party allowed in Russia was the Communist Party.

Pulling Russia out of the First World War

Lenin hoped the Germans and Austrians would make peace without asking too much of Russia. But he was to be disappointed. When the three countries met at **Brest-Litovsk** in December 1917, it became clear that Russia would have to make huge sacrifices to buy peace.

Source A

- Talks to end the war to begin at once.

- Land owned by the Tsar, church and nobility to be given to the people.

- Religious teaching to stop.

- Women to be seen as equal to men.

- All titles, except 'Citizen' and 'Comrade' to be abolished.

- Factory workers to work no more than 8 hours a day.

- All non-Bolshevik newspapers to be closed.

▲ **Decrees issued by the Bolsheviks between November 1917 and March 1918.**

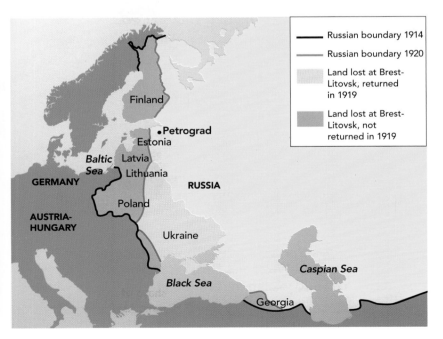

◀ **Land lost by Russia under the Treaty of Brest-Litovsk, 1918.**

Russian boundary 1914
Russian boundary 1920
Land lost at Brest-Litovsk, returned in 1919
Land lost at Brest-Litovsk, not returned in 1919

Finland
Petrograd
Estonia
Baltic Sea
Latvia
Lithuania
GERMANY
RUSSIA
Poland
AUSTRIA-HUNGARY
Ukraine
Caspian Sea
Black Sea
Georgia

The price of peace

Lenin sent **Trotsky**, the Minister of Foreign Affairs (see page 29), to Brest-Litovsk to negotiate for Russia. Trotsky was appalled by the German and Austrian demands. But Lenin was determined to end the war at any price. He knew Russia was on the point of civil war. It would be impossible for his government to fight the Germans and the Whites.

On 3 March 1918, the government signed the **Treaty of Brest-Litovsk**. The treaty made Russia pay a huge fine to Germany for the cost of the war. Russia also had to hand over to Germany and Austria-Hungary the following lands: Finland, Estonia, Latvia, Lithuania, Poland, Georgia and the Ukraine.

The territory lost by Russia included some of its most valuable land and industrial areas. The rich farming lands of the Ukraine and the rich industrial areas around the Baltic were two major sacrifices made to win peace. The treaty made many Russians (including Bolsheviks) furious, but Lenin believed that these sacrifices had to be made to save the revolution.

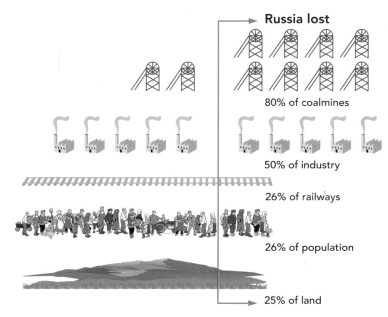

Russia lost

80% of coalmines

50% of industry

26% of railways

26% of population

25% of land

▲ **Russian losses in the Treaty of Brest-Litovsk, 1918.**

SUMMARY

Establishing Communist Government

1917	7-8 November	Bolsheviks seize power in Petrograd.
	November	Telegrams sent to rest of Russia.
		Sovnarkom set up.
1918	18 January	Constituent Assembly dissolved.
	February	Bolshevik Party changes name.
	onwards	Reforms introduced.
	3 March	Russia left the First World War.
		Treaty of Brest-Litovsk.

BOCHKAREVA (1899–?)

Maria Bochkareva was sent out to work at the age of eight. She married young, but the marriage was not a happy one. In 1914 her husband tried to kill her. She left home to join the army.

Bochkareva was a brave fighter and won many medals. In 1917 she set up the Women's Death Battalion in Petrograd, to shame men into joining the army. She later fell out with the Bolsheviks and was sentenced to death. She fled to the USA.

Shortly after the signing of the Treaty of Brest-Litovsk, civil war broke out. Lenin's government (the **Reds**) was opposed by the **Whites**.

Who were the Whites?

The Whites were made up of many different groups. Some of them wanted the Tsar back. Some wanted a government like the old Provisional Government. Some (like the Cossacks in the Ukraine) wanted independence from Russia. Some (capitalists or landowners) opposed the Reds for financial reasons.

One unusual White group was the **Czech Legion** made up of 45,000 Czechoslovakian prisoners of war. While being taken home, fighting broke out and the Legion took over the Trans-Siberian railway, a vital link between east and west Russia.

Foreign powers helped the Whites too. They were opposed to the Reds because they did not want communist ideas to spread to their countries.

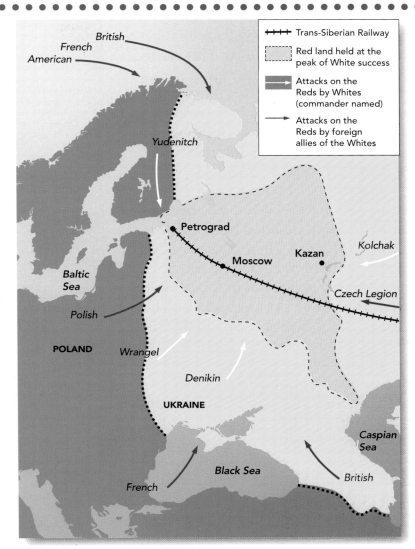

▲ The Civil War in Russia 1918–21.

Source B

England, America and France are fighting Russia. They want revenge for the Soviet Union's overthrow of the landowners and capitalists. They are helping the Russian landowners with money and military supplies. The landowners are attacking Soviet power. They want to restore the Tsar, landowners and capitalists. But no! This shall never be.

▲ Part of a speech by Lenin in 1919.

Foreign aid for the Whites

Russia's old allies were angry with Lenin for pulling out of the war. Then his government refused to pay back all the money they had lent the Tsar. This, added to their fear that communist ideas would spread to their countries, led them to support the White armies. At one stage in the Civil War, the Reds were fighting the Whites and also fourteen different foreign countries on six separate fronts.

In the spring of 1919, White troops under General **Kolchak** invaded eastern Russia and reached Kazan. Then Whites under General **Deniken** moved from the Ukraine to within 300 km of Moscow. Trotsky drove their armies back. Kolchak was later captured and executed. Deniken resigned and his army disbanded. In the early summer of 1919, another White leader, General **Yudenitch**, attacked from the north and threatened Petrograd. But by the end of the year, he too had been defeated.

As the White armies suffered defeats, foreign powers began to withdraw. Then the Poles (supporting the Whites) launched a surprise invasion in 1920 and captured Kiev. In June 1920, a White army led by General **Wrangel** attacked from the south, hoping to link up with the Poles. But the Poles made peace with the Reds, and Wrangel had to withdraw.

Victory for the Reds

Some Japanese forces in the east were not defeated until 1922, but the peace treaty with Poland (the Treaty of Riga) is seen by most historians as the end of the Civil War. Despite all opposition, the Communist Red Army had won.

▲ A Communist poster of 1918 showing the Red Army fighting the many-headed monster of the Whites. One of the heads is Tsar Nicholas.

KOLCHAK (1873–1920)

Kolchak fought in the Russo-Japanese War and commanded the Black Sea Fleet during the First World War. After the November Revolution he set up an anti Bolshevik government at Omsk (in Siberia), calling himself 'Supreme Ruler of all Russia'. After his troops were defeated he was captured by the Bolsheviks and shot on 7 February 1920.

Just before the November Revolution, the Bolsheviks had deliberately weakened the Russian army. They had encouraged soldiers to desert. They had demanded the removal of the death penalty for offences in the army. And they had pushed for army officers to be elected.

1 Trotsky and the Red Army

When the Civil War broke out, the Bolsheviks paid a price for their actions. They needed an efficient, well-disciplined army to defeat the Whites. And they needed it quickly. Trotsky was given the job of raising this army. In March 1918, he was made Chairman of the **Supreme War Council**. It was Trotsky's brilliant organization that led to the victory of the Reds in the Civil War.

Source E

The military specialists [former officers in the Tsar's army] will be watched. Any who shows signs of betraying Soviet Russia will be shot. Next to every specialist should be a commissar [a loyal Bolshevik], to the right, and to the left, revolver in hand.

▲ Part of Trotsky's speech to the Central Executive Committee on 29 July 1918. Trotsky knew that he needed the experienced officers of the Tsar to run the army. He had no time to train loyal Bolsheviks to do the job. But he knew the Tsar's officers would have to be forced to help.

▼ A Communist poster praising the three million strong Red Army.

Source D

ДА ЗДРАВСТВУЕТ КРАСНАЯ 3х МИЛЛИОННАЯ АРМИЯ!!

Building the Red Army

Many men joined the Red Army when they saw that soldiers were better fed than most civilians. But more troops were needed. So Trotsky used **conscription**. All men aged 18–40 were forced to join the army. But this hugh force needed experienced officers to lead the mostly inexperienced men. So Trotsky used officers from the Tsar's army, and threatened to shoot them if they did not obey. Sometimes their families were taken hostage to make sure they obeyed.

Trotsky appointed party members (**commissars**) to help run the army. There was a commissar responsible for troop morale, and one for troop training. Trotsky used harsh discipline, but was a fine leader.

White troops, on the other hand, were badly led and had no common aim. They were fighting over such a huge area it was hard to co-ordinate attacks. Whites had little peasant support, but they had foreign help. So the Communists could say they were fighting against foreign invaders and so appeal to Russian patriotism.

Source F

Trotsky visited the front lines. He made a speech. We were lifted by his energy. The situation, which had been catastrophic 24 hours earlier, had improved by his coming as though by miracle.

▲ A Red Army soldier's description of the effect of Trotsky's leadership on troops at Gomel in 1918.

Source G

The state police of the Tsar throttled the workers who were fighting to set up a socialist state. Our Cheka shoots landlords, capitalists and generals who are trying to restore the capitalist way of life.

▲ Trotsky replying in 1920 to the accusation that the Cheka were no different to the Tsar's Okhrana.

2 The 'Red Terror'

The Communists had many opponents in 1917, so they had to crush opposition quickly. In December 1917, Lenin set up the **Cheka** to deal with law and order and political opposition. In 1918, the Cheka began the 'Red Terror'. People suspected of being against the revolution were arrested, tortured and executed. In August 1918, an attempt to assassinate Lenin almost succeeded, so the Cheka stepped up its terror campaign. In Petrograd alone, over 800 'enemies of the state' were executed. By the end of the Civil War some 200,000 people had been killed and 85,000 locked away.

3 War communism

Lenin introduced **war communism** during the Civil War. This meant that the government took over the economy to make sure the Red Army had the weapons and food it needed. This kept the army supplied, but led to widespread starvation for the peasants and workers of Russia.

Under war communism, private trading was banned. It was seen to be wrong to make a profit. Factories with more than ten workers were taken over by the government. Strikes were made illegal.

Peasant resentment

In the countryside, peasants were encouraged to work harder still. The surplus crops they grew were taken to feed factory workers and the army. The peasants resented this. The Communists had given them the right to own their land, and they wanted to profit from it by selling their crops.

Using less money

The government also abolished money charges on services like railways and the post. They did this to encourage **bartering** (swapping goods) instead of using money. As inflation made the rouble almost worthless, many peasants did swap goods instead of using money.

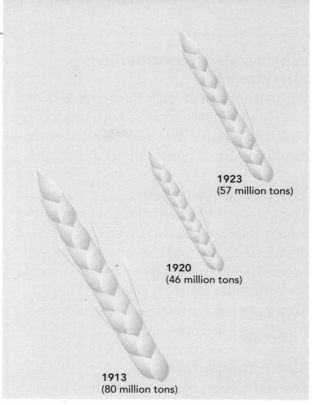

1923
(57 million tons)

1920
(46 million tons)

1913
(80 million tons)

▲ The decline in grain production in Russia 1913–23.

▼ Victims of the famine in Russia in 1921.

Source *H*

Why was war communism abandoned?

War communism kept the army and the factory workers supplied with food. It was vital during the Civil War. But it also made the Communist government unpopular.

The peasants resist

The peasants resented the government taking their spare crops. Many of them decided to grow only as much as they needed. Others hid any spare food so the government collectors could not find it. Many peasants attacked the government collectors when they arrived.

Not enough food

The unrest and slowing down of food production meant that there were growing food shortages. In 1921, there was a terrible famine. Millions died.

The Kronstadt mutiny

In March 1921, the sailors at the Kronstadt naval base mutinied. These sailors had supported the November Revolution. But now they felt that Lenin's government had not kept its promises. The uprising was a serious threat to the government. Trotsky took an army of 60,000 men to deal with the sailors. Thousands of the rebels were killed and many more arrested. But 10,000 Red Army soldiers also died in the fighting.

Source I

▲ A Communist poster from 1920 (the year before the Kronstadt mutiny) praising naval help in the revolution.

SUMMARY

The Communists win the fight for survival

▶ 1918   Trotsky created the Red Army.

War communism supplied army.

Duma dissolved.

Cheka imposed Red Terror.

▶ 1919   Whites defeated on battlefield.

▶ 1920   Foreign powers withdraw.

Kronstadt mutiny.

▶ 1921   War communism abandoned.

KOLLONTAI (1872–1952)

Alexandra Kollontai was born in St. Petersburg. She wrote radical pamphlets supporting the rights of women and factory workers. She was forced to flee by the Tsar's secret police.

Kollontai joined the Bolsheviks and toured the USA making speeches supporting Bolshevik ideas. She returned to Russia after the March Revolution and Lenin made her Commissar for Public Welfare in his government. Stalin kept her in his government. He made her Minister for Norway and, later, Ambassador to Sweden.

The New Economic Policy

The government was losing popularity, even with people who had once supported it. Lenin had seen this happen to the Provisional Government. He knew that the Communists had to change their harsh economic policy to win back the support of the peasants and workers.

In March 1921, Lenin introduced the **New Economic Policy (NEP)**. By doing this, Lenin showed he accepted that not all communist ideas could be introduced at once. He was prepared to take a step back to win the support of the people. The following concessions were made in the New Economic Policy:

1 The government stopped taking surplus crops. Peasants who managed to grow more food than they needed could sell any surplus for a profit. The government put a 10% tax on these profits. This tax had to be paid in crops.

2 The government kept control of all large industries. But factories with fewer than twenty workers were returned to private ownership and could be run to make a profit.

3 Anyone could open a shop to sell or hire goods for profit.

4 Bartering was discouraged. The government encouraged people to use money again.

Opposition to the NEP

Many Communists opposed the NEP because they said it went against communist beliefs. Encouraging profit-making was a step back to the evil of capitalism. But Lenin argued that there was no choice. Like the Treaty of Brest-Litovsk, the NEP was a sacrifice which he felt had to be made for the Communists to stay in power. Lenin also stressed that the NEP was a temporary measure. The government would regain its control of the economy when it was more secure.

Source J

We are now going back, but we will retreat first only to run forward more strongly. We retreated when we introduced our New Economic Policy, but we knew we would begin a more determined offensive after the retreat.

▲ Part of a speech made by Lenin in 1921, explaining why the New Economic Policy was introduced.

▼ The effects of the NEP (official government figures).

1922	77.7 hectares sown	50.3 million tons	0.2 tons
1923	91.7 hectares sown	50.6 million tons	0.3 tons
1924	98.1 hectares sown	51.4 million tons	0.8 tons
1925	104.3 hectares sown	72.5 million tons	1.5 tons
1926	110.3 hectares sown	76.8 million tons	2.4 tons

Did the NEP work?

In one way, the NEP was highly successful. The peasants and workers were happier and produced more food and goods. But farms were small and inefficient (compared with other European countries). The NEP also created a situation where some peasants grew rich by selling surplus crops. They became known as **Kulaks**. They began to hire poorer peasants to work for them. So Lenin's policy allowed a capitalist class of peasants to develop. This was against communist beliefs. It also meant that the Kulaks would be against any future agricultural reform – as Stalin was to discover in 1929 (see page 51).

(see page 51).

Source K

The men made by the New Economic Policy (small shop-keepers, traders, all anti-Communist) improved overall living standards enough for the Bolsheviks to survive. But in return the Bolsheviks killed off the NEP and the NEP men.

▲ Brian Moynahan, in *The Russian Century*, 1994.

5.5 How did Russia become the Soviet Union?

● ●

In July 1918, the Communist government drew up a new constitution. It set up the **Russian Socialist Federal Soviet Republic**. This made the All-Russian Congress of Soviets the most important group in the country. They would elect a committee of 200 members, which would elect the **Council of People's Commissars**. These people would run the country. The government also moved from Petrograd to Moscow. Despite the new constitution, Lenin still made all the decisions.

In 1924, Russia changed its name to the **Union of Soviet Socialist Republics** (known in the west as the USSR or Soviet Union). The country was set up as a union of four republics: Russia, the Ukraine, Byelorussia and the Caucasus. Each ran local matters, like education. Foreign policy and the armed forces were controlled by the government.

Source L

▶ A Russian poster from November 1918, celebrating one year of Bolshevik government. Through the window can be seen the dream of a productive communist Russia. The worker and peasant are standing on symbols representing the evils of the past.

CHKHEIDZEI (1864–1926)

Nikolai Chkheidzei was a Social Democrat who was a member of the first Duma (of 1907) and became President of the Petrograd Soviet. He disapproved of the Bolshevik takeover. He tried to set up an independent republic in Georgia, but failed. He fled to France in 1921.

The death of Lenin

During 1922 and 1923, Lenin had several heart attacks. In January 1924, he died. For a week after his death, thousands of mourners queued in the freezing weather to pay their last respects.

Lenin the hero?

After the funeral, Lenin's body was not buried or cremated. It was embalmed (preserved) and put in a specially built tomb in Moscow. Petrograd, where the November Revolution had broken out, was renamed **Leningrad**. Many Russians (and historians) see Lenin as a hero. But others believe that this view of Lenin as the saviour of the Russian people is exaggerated.

Source 1

Of all the tyrannies in history, the Bolshevik tyranny is the worst. The atrocities committed under Lenin and Trotsky are much more hideous (and more numerous) than anything the Kaiser (the German ruler during the war) has done.

▲ Speech made by Winston Churchill, British Secretary for War and Air, at the end of the First World War.

Source 3

▲ A poster of Lenin published by the Soviet government in 1967.

Source 2

▲ A picture painted during Lenin's lifetime showing him meeting leaders of people of eastern Russia. In the background are Trostky and Dzerhinsky.

Source 4

It seemed as if one dictatorship (that of the Tsars) had simply been replaced by that of Lenin and his Communist Party. A one-party state, a secret police and a 'party' army did not look like much of a change to most Russians.

▲ A modern historian commenting on the situation in Russia in 1918.

Source 5

ТОВ. Ленин ОЧИЩАЕТ
землю от нечисти.

▲ A poster issued by Lenin's government showing him sweeping away the royal family, nobles, the Church and capitalists. It is entitled *'Lenin Cleans the Earth of Evil Spirits'*.

Source 7

► Part of an article written by Lenin's widow. It was printed in the party newspaper, *Pravda*, shortly after his death.

Do not build memorials to him, name palaces after him, or hold celebrations in his memory. All of this meant so little to him.

Source 8

Lenin was one of the most sinister figures ever. This evil man was the founder and mainstay of Bolshevism.

It is a great mistake to look upon him as a moderate. He was a revolutionary whose thirst for power could never be satisfied.

► Extract from the British newspaper, the *Morning Post*, in 1924.

Source 6

When he spoke, complete silence fell over the hall. All eyes were on him. Comrade Lenin looked at the crowd as if casting a spell over it.

I watched the big audience. I did not see a single person move or cough in three hours. Comrade Lenin is the greatest speaker I have ever heard.

▲ Said by Katayama, organizer of the Japanese Communist Party, who went to hear a speech made by Lenin in 1921.

Was Lenin a 'Red Tyrant'?

Lenin was seen as a great hero in the Soviet Union. He had helped to organize the Bolshevik Party and led the 1917 Revolution. He had defeated the Communists' enemies and started to introduce communist reforms. This image is seen quite clearly in Sources 2 and 3.

But to Russia's political opponents (like Winston Churchill in Source 1) Lenin was no better than the Tsar. The Russian people still had to face hardship and lack of political freedom.

Tyrants force their people to obey them. Did Lenin use force, or were the Russian people prepared to suffer in the cause of a fairer social system? The sources on this page give a variety of opinions to help you to decide what you think.

CHAPTER 6

STALIN AND THE MODERNIZATION OF THE SOVIET UNION

▲ A painting of Lenin speaking with Stalin sitting by his side. The painting, entitled *Comrade-in-arms at the First All-Russian Congress of Soviets, June 1917* was painted after Lenin's death.

When Lenin died in 1924, there was a struggle for power. By 1929, Stalin had won. Stalin wanted to modernize the Soviet Union. He feared the west would attack, and he wanted the Soviet Union to be able to resist. Despite fierce opposition, he set up **collective farming** and a series of **Five Year Plans** to improve Soviet industries. In 1941, **Nazi Germany** invaded. The Soviet Union beat back the invasion, though only after terrible sacrifices.

Stalin was determined to wipe out any opposition. Millions of Soviet citizens died in his **'purges'**. It was little wonder that Stalin's cruelty was attacked by his successor, Khrushchev, in 1956.

6.1 Why did Stalin take over after Lenin's death?

Who will run the Soviet Union?

When Lenin died in 1924, many people thought Trotsky would take over. Trotsky had been vital in winning the Civil War. He was an excellent speaker. But he was also arrogant and bad tempered, so he was unpopular in the Communist Party. Lenin had warned his colleagues that Trotsky was over-confident.

Immediately after Lenin's death, the seven members of the **Politburo** (the ruling body of the Communist Party) ran the country between them. They spent most of their time locked in a struggle for the leadership. Two serious contenders emerged – Trotsky and Stalin.

MEMBERS OF THE POLITBURO IN 1924

Trotsky:	Commissar for War
Stalin:	Communist Party Secretary
Kamenev:	Chairman of the Politburo
Rykov:	Chairman of Sovnarkom
Zinoviev:	Chairman of Comintern*
Bukharin:	responsible for propaganda
Tomsky:	responsible for trade unions

An organization set up in 1919 to help Communists in other countries

Stalin plots for power

Stalin was Secretary of the Party. This meant he could affect who got important Party jobs. While Trotsky had been away fighting the Civil War, Stalin had been in Petrograd, being friendly to everyone, including Lenin.

Lenin did not like Stalin and did not think he would be a good leader. He made this clear in a letter to the Party known as a postscript to his *Testament*. But when Lenin died, the *Testament* had not been made public. Stalin knew how important it was to have a good image. He made sure he had an important part in the funeral ceremony. Trotsky was not at the funeral at all. He was in southern Russia (recovering from malaria) when Lenin died. He later said he phoned Moscow to find out when the funeral was, and that Stalin gave him the wrong date. As Trotsky and Stalin became bitter rivals, it is easy to believe this story. It is equally possible that Trotsky made it up to show Stalin in a poor light.

Source C

Comrade Stalin, as Secretary, has unlimited authority and I am not sure if he will be able to use it carefully enough.

Comrade Trotsky, on the other hand, is distinguished not only by his outstanding ability. He is perhaps the most capable man in the present Committee – but he has displayed excessive self-assurance.

▲ Lenin's views on Stalin and Trotsky, as set out in a letter he wrote to the Party just before his death. The letter has become known as his *Testament*.

Source B

Stalin is too rude. This fault is intolerable in a Secretary. I propose to comrades that they find a way of removing Stalin and appointing another man who is more patient, more loyal, more polite and is considerate to his comrades.

▲ A postscript to Lenin's *Testament*, written ten days after the main letter.

Source D

► Lenin making a speech in 1920. The two men standing beside the rostrum are Trotsky and Kamenev. When this photograph was published again (after Stalin came to power), Trotsky and Kamenev were no longer in the picture.

Stalin or Trotsky?

One of the major differences between Trotsky and Stalin was their view on how communist ideas should be spread. **Trotsky** believed that communism could not survive in the Soviet Union unless communism spread to other countries. He said the Soviet Union had to help to start communist revolutions everywhere.

Stalin believed that the Soviet Union should work to make itself a modern and powerful communist country. It should think about being able to protect itself against the world, rather than starting a world-wide revolution.

Stalin had the support of Kamenev and Zinoviev (see page 45). Between them, they made sure that Trotsky did not take over as leader. Also, Zinoviev and Kamenev persuaded the other members of the Politburo not to expel Stalin or embarrass him by making Lenin's *Testament* public.

Easing out Trotsky

From 1924, Trotsky lost more and more of his jobs in the Party. In 1929, he was exiled from the Soviet Union.

Easing out the rest

Now Stalin did not need Zinoviev and Kamenev any longer. So he had them expelled from the Politburo. By the end of 1929, Stalin had also forced Bukharin, Rykov and Tomsky to resign from the Politburo, which was now full of his own supporters. The battle for the leadership was over. Stalin was now firmly in control in the Soviet Union.

Source E

As for Trotsky, he was a coward during the Brest-Litovsk negotiations. The greatest victories in the Civil War were won in spite of him. Trotsky had no special role in the Party, in the uprising or in the October days, as he was relatively new in our party.

▲ **Part of a speech made by Stalin in 1924.**

THE DOWNFALL OF TROTSKY

▶ **1925** Resigned as Commissar for War.
▶ **1926** Expelled from Politburo.
▶ **1927** Expelled from Communist Party.
▶ **1928** Deported to Soviet Central Asia.
▶ **1929** Exiled from the Soviet Union.

ZINOVIEV (1883–1936)

Zinoviev joined the Social Democrats in 1901 and became a firm supporter of Lenin. He was active in the 1905 Revolution and was forced into exile from 1905–17. In 1917 Zinoviev returned to Russia. He became Chairman of the Leningrad Soviet, a member of the Politburo and (from 1919–26) Chairman of the Executive Committee of the Comintern.

After Lenin's death, Stalin saw Zinoviev as a serious rival. He had Zinoviev expelled from the Party. In 1935 he was sentenced to 10 years' imprisonment for supposed involvement in Kirov's murder. He was re-tried in 1936 and executed.

A backward industry

When Stalin came to power, the economy of the Soviet Union was way behind countries like Britain, Germany and the United States. Stalin wanted the Soviet Union to be able to compete with other nations. He feared it would not survive otherwise. In 1921, Lenin had set up the State Planning Commission (**Gosplan**). Stalin used it to change the Soviet Union into a major industrial power.

Five Year Plans

In 1928, Gosplan came up with its **first Five Year Plan**. It set targets for industry, power supply and transport. Each group of workers had a set of production targets to aim for. The targets were often too high, but workers were offered rewards to meet them. Those who failed were likely to be fined, or even lose their jobs.

Punishments and rewards

Russian factory workers were not used to aiming for high productivity. In the early 1930s, many workers were peasants who had moved to the towns. They were used to working at their own speed, not as fast as possible. So the government laid down strict rules for workers. Workers who took time off could lose their jobs and their homes. Their ration cards were taken away, making it hard to buy food.

Under the Five Year Plan, workers who reached their targets were paid higher wages. But most targets were too high. In 1929, the government said factories must work seven days a week to produce more. Many workers found factory work too demanding, so they went to find work somewhere else. In 1932, the government introduced internal passports. Workers now needed permission to move around.

Source F

To slacken the pace would mean to lag behind, and those who lag behind are beaten. We do not want to be beaten. We are 50–100 years behind the advanced countries. We must make good this lag in ten years. Either we do it, or they crush us.

▲ Part of a speech made by Stalin in 1931.

Source G

▲ 'We Smite the Lazy Workers'.
A Soviet poster from 1931.
Smite means to strike someone down.

The Stakhanovite movement

Some younger workers set up **shock brigades**, which tried to beat previous production levels. They were given more pay and better housing. Some of the very best workers were given medals. They were called Stakhanovites after Alexei Stakhanov, a miner. In 1934, Stakhanov was said to have organized his fellow workers to cut 102 tons of coal in a single shift. The target for the shift was just 7 tons. Stakhanov became a national hero.

But the Stakhanovites were hated by their fellow workers. As harsh targets and constant propaganda began to make workers resentful, so the Stakhanovite movement was no longer promoted by the government.

Source H

▲ A posed propaganda photograph of Alexei Stakhanov explaining his methods to other workers.

Labour camps

These were set up by the government and did two jobs. They punished opponents of the government and they provided a huge workforce that could be pushed far harder than ordinary workers. They were filled with opponents of Stalin's régime, ranging from peasants who had fought **collectivization** (see page 52) to intellectuals and writers who criticized the government. Stalin said these people would be 'cleansed' of their anti-social views by useful work. They built roads, bridges and canals.

The camps were run by a unit of the secret police called **Gulag**. The Soviet **dissident** (government critic) Alexander Solzhenitsyn spent many years in them. Much of what we know about them comes from his writings. He talks about people freezing to death in temperatures so low that the mercury in the thermometers froze. Living conditions were appalling and there was never enough food.

In 1928, there were about 30,000 labour camp prisoners. By 1938, it was about 7,000,000. No-one knows the exact number of deaths in the labour camps, but during Stalin's rule it may well have been as high as 12,000,000.

Source I

Corpses were left on the work site at the end of the day. At night the sledges fetched them back.

In the summer you saw the bones of corpses which had not been removed. They went into the concrete mixer with the shingle. So, as part of the concrete, they will be preserved for ever.

▲ Part of a book by Russian dissident writer Alexander Solzhenitsyn, *The Gulag Archipelago*, 1974.

The second Five Year Plan

In 1929, Stalin said the first Five Year Plan would reach its production levels in just four years. In 1932, a second Five Year Plan was drawn up. It was supposed to concentrate on tractors for collective farms (see page 52) and factory tools and machinery. But its main focus was really war goods, because Stalin was more and more certain that war would break out with Nazi Germany.

The third and fourth Five Year Plans

The third Five Year Plan began in 1938. Its main focus was household goods and luxuries like radios and bicycles. It also aimed to improve the quality of goods – almost 40% of goods produced in the first two plans were faulty. In 1941, Nazi Germany invaded the Soviet Union, and the plan had to be stopped. A fourth Five Year Plan was introduced in 1946 to rebuild the country after the war. This was a great success.

The effects of the Five Year Plans

In just ten years, the Soviet Union became the second largest industrial power in the world. Huge new steel plants, hydro-electric power stations, railways and canals were built. Vast numbers of factories in hundreds of new towns poured out manufactured goods. Between 1928 and 1932, the tiny village of Magnitogorsk in the Urals became an industrial city with over 25,000,000 citizens. This happened all over the Soviet Union. Stalin had also, by planning ahead, enabled the Soviet Union to resist the German invasion.

Source J

	1928	1932	1937
Coal	36	66	139
Iron	3	6	15
Steel	4	6	18
Oil	12	23	29

▲ The growth of Soviet industry 1928–37. Figures given are output in million tons.

Source K

By May the whole city was swimming in mud. Plague had broken out not far away. The resistance of the people was low because of lack of food and overwork.

Sanitary conditions were appalling. By the middle of May the heat had become intolerable.

▲ Description of the working conditions in Magnitogorsk by J. Scott, an American engineer.

JOE SCOTT

Joe Scott was an American who was inspired by the ideals of the Russian Revolution. A graduate of Wisconsin University, he trained as a welder and went to Russia as a volunteer at the gigantic iron and steel works being set up at Magnitogorsk in 1929. He wanted to join 'a society that was at least one step in front of America,' he said. His diary gives the point of view of a sympathetic outsider. He was stunned by the harsh conditions, under which 'men froze, hungered and suffered, and by the spirit with which the work went on with a complete disregard for individual and personal considerations.'

SUMMARY

The Modernization of Soviet Industry

▶ 1921 Gosplan set up.

▶ 1928 First Five Year Plan.

   Strict targets set.

   Control of working practices.

   Labour camps.

▶ 1932 Second Five Year Plan.

▶ 1938 Third Five Year Plan.

▶ 1946 Fourth Five Year Plan.

If Soviet industry was to develop rapidly, the workers in the city had to be well-fed. But the NEP was not producing enough food.

Inefficient methods

The Soviet system of farming was wildly inefficient. Most peasants owned tiny pieces of land which they cultivated by the old **strip farming** system. Many of them were too poor to afford modern equipment. Even in the late 1920s, most peasants used a horse-drawn wooden plough not a tractor.

The Kulak problem

The NEP had created a class of richer peasants, the Kulaks (see page 42. They resented having to sell extra crops to the government at a low price. By 1927, Stalin had seen that Soviet agriculture had to be modernized. And something had to be done about the Kulaks.

Source M

▲ A group of Soviet peasants carrying a banner with the inscription 'We demand collectivization and the wiping out of all Kulaks'.

Source L

Isn't it time you stopped thinking each one for himself? You Kulaks, of course, will never accept a new order. You love to fatten on other people's blood. But we know how to deal with you. We'll wipe you off the face of the earth.

▲ Part of a government official's speech to a group of villagers, telling them why they should join a collective farm.

Source N

Look at the Kulak farms: their barns and sheds are crammed with grain. They are waiting for prices to rise. So long as there are Kulaks, our towns and industrial centres, as well as our Red Army, will be poorly supplied and will be threatened with hunger. We cannot allow that.

We must break this class, abolish it. This is necessary to be able to stop importing grain and to save foreign currency for the development of industry.

▲ Extracts from speeches made by Stalin in 1928 and 1929 about collectivization.

A political embarassment

The Kulaks had always embarrassed the government. Communist ideas did not allow for individual profit-making. Lenin had been forced to introduce the NEP, which had produced the Kulaks. But Stalin decided the Kulaks had to go.

Famine

By 1928, he could see starvation looming in the cities. He sent the army to enforce 'grain procurement' (buying up grain at very low prices). Then he introduced rationing in the cities. Even these measures did not solve the problem.

Collectivization

So, in 1929, Stalin announced that Soviet farming was to be **collectivized**. This meant that all fields, machinery and animals were to be used to set up **collective farms (Kolkhozs)** which would be farmed by whole villages, not individual farmers. These would be much more efficient than the tiny farms. Motor Tractor Stations would be set up to supply the collective farms with tractors. Peasants were told they could keep small plots of land by their cottages. They would be paid wages and the crops would be sold to the government at a low price. Crops could no longer be sold for a profit.

The end of the Kulaks

Stalin knew collectivization would be extremely unpopular with the Kulaks. So he sent officials into the countryside to persuade the peasants to accept collectivization. But many of them still refused to join the collective farms, so the government used force. The Red Army and the state police arrested and deported millions of peasants. Most of the estimated 5,000,000 Kulaks were exiled to remote parts of the country or sent to labour camps, where many of them died.

Source O

КУЛАКИ САМЫЕ ЗВЕРСКИЕ, САМЫЕ ГРУБЫЕ, САМЫЕ ДИКИЕ, ЭКСПЛОАТАТОРЫ, НЕ РАЗ ВОССТАНАВЛИВАВШИЕ В ИСТОРИИ ДРУГИХ СТРАН ВЛАСТЬ ПОМЕЩИКОВ, ЦАРЕЙ, ПОПОВ...И КАПИТАЛИСТОВ.
ЛЕНИН.

ДОЛОЙ КУЛАКА ИЗ КОЛХОЗА

▲ A government poster of a Kulak.

Source P

Millions of peasants, rather than give them up to the collectives, killed their cows, sheep, and chickens. For a short time, Russians ate more meat than they had for decades. Then they went on a vegetarian diet.

▲ An American newspaper reporter describing what he saw in the Soviet Union in 1930.

Food shortages and starvation

The peasants did not give up without a fight. Many of them killed their animals and destroyed their crops rather than give them to the collectives. In 1932–3, the Soviet Union suffered a terrible famine and there was widespread starvation. Food shortages were so bad that cannibalism was reported. Some historians say as many as 10,000,000 peasants died. While people starved, Stalin sold grain to other countries to make money for materials and machinery for Soviet industry.

Did collectivization work?

Despite the terrible problems of the early 1930s, collectivization was a success in the end. Stalin ruthlessly broke the Kulaks and forced the peasants into Kolkhozs. By 1937, over 90% of peasant farms had been collectivized and the Kulaks had been destroyed.

From 1933, Soviet agricultural production improved. More and more peasants had tractors. Their lives were improved in other ways too. The government set up schemes to improve literacy on the farms. Stalin had brought about a revolution in agriculture, in much the same way that he had revolutionized industry.

Source R

УДАРИМ ПО КУЛАКУ

АГИТИРУЮЩЕМУ ЗА СОКРАЩЕНИЕ ПОСЕВА

▲ A government poster showing an anti-social Kulak guarding his plot while tractors cultivate collective land all around him.

SOLZHENITSYN (1918–)

Alexander Solzhenitsyn graduated from Rostov University in 1941. He joined the Red Army, but was arrested for criticizing Stalin.

Solzhenitsyn wrote *One Day in the Life of Ivan Denisovich*, which gave a damning picture of life in Stalin's labour camps. It was published in 1962 (after Stalin's death) and made Solzhenitsyn an international hero. He was expelled from Russia after his novel *Gulag Archipelago* was critical of the new government.

Source Q

Number of livestock in the Soviet Union 1928–33 (Figures are in millions).

	1928	1929	1930	1931	1932	1933
Cattle	71	67	53	48	41	38
Pigs	26	20	14	14	12	12
Sheep and goats	147	147	109	78	52	50

6.4 How did Stalin deal with opposition in the Soviet Union?

Purges

Stalin's policies of collectivization and industrialization had made him many opponents. During the 1930s, Stalin became more and more concerned about this. He decided to deal with anyone he thought was against him. He set up 'purges' to eliminate 'enemies of the state'. Between 1936 and 1953, over 40,000,000 people were arrested. About 24,000,000 of them were executed or died in labour camps.

Many of the 'purged' were loyal Communists with years of service to the Party. Often they could not believe what was happening to them. Most of Stalin's victims were ordinary people like teachers and factory workers, who had made the authorities suspicious of them. Few of the victims actually wanted to overthrow communism or replace Stalin with the exiled Trotsky.

People have given various explanations for Stalin's purges. Some historians say Stalin had so many enemies that he thought everyone was out to get him. Others say that mass arrests and exile to labour camps were the only way Stalin could find a labour force to work in the harsher parts of the Soviet Union.

Source T

Supporters of Trotsky and Zinoviev worked for the defeat of the Soviet Union to restore capitalism. Trotsky, Zinoviev and Kamenev have been in conspiracy against Lenin, the Party and the Soviet state ever since the October Revolution.

▲ Stalin writing in his *History of the Communist Party of the Soviet Union* in 1939.

Source U

Many Bolsheviks who were arrested simply refused to believe Stalin knew what was going on, let alone had ordered it to happen.

They wrote to him. Some of them, after being tortured, inscribed 'Long live Stalin' in blood on the walls of their prison.

▲ The poet Yevtushenko remembers the time of the purges in his autobiography. He describes Stalin's popularity despite the cruelty and injustice of the purges.

Source S

VISITEZ L.U.R.S.S. SES PYRAMIDES!...

◄ A cartoon published in Paris in the 1930s. Its caption says 'Visit the Pyramids of the USSR'.

Show trials

The purges began after the assassination of Sergei Kirov in December 1934. Kirov was a member of the **Politburo**, and the circumstances of his death are very suspicious. Stalin's state police seem to have known about the plot to kill Kirov. Some Soviet historians believe Stalin let Kirov die because he was a possible rival, and his death gave Stalin an excuse to act against political opponents.

Stalin accused two Party members, Kamenev and Zinoviev (see pages 45 and 47) of involvement in Kirov's assassination and plotting against Stalin. They were arrested and given long prison sentences. Then, in 1936, Kamenev, Zinoviev and fourteen others were accused of conspiring with Trotsky to overthrow the government. They all confessed and were executed. Their trial was the first of the **show trials** in which leading Communists confessed to crimes involving trying to overthrow the government.

A real threat?

Most of the crimes that people were accused of involved supporting Trotsky in attempts to overthrow Stalin. Few, if any, of these people were guilty. They were often tortured into confessing, or told that their families would be hurt if they did not confess. As well as those who were tried in show trials, thousands of other Party members were executed or sent to labour camps.

Source V

▲ A cartoon from an American newspaper in the 1930s.

Source W

The judge asked 'Don't you know that Kirov was killed in Leningrad?' I replied 'Yes, but it wasn't I who killed him, it was someone called Nikolayev. And I've never been to Leningrad in my life.'

The judge snapped 'You've never been to Leningrad, but Kirov was killed by people with your ideas, so you share the responsibility'.

The officials 'withdrew for consultation', but were back within two minutes. The judge had a sheet of paper in his hand that must have taken 20 minutes to type. The judge announced the verdict. 'Ten years maximum isolation in prison'.

▲ Eugenia Ginzburg, a university lecturer, describes her seven minute trial for alleged involvement in the murder of Kirov. As a result of the trial, she served eighteen years in a labour camp.

Source X

I am fully and utterly guilty of being the organizer, second only to Trotsky, of the group whose task was the killing of Stalin.

▲ Part of the confession made by Zinoviev in his trial.

Source Y

Lenin's General Staff of 1917

STALIN, THE EXECUTIONER, ALONE REMAINS

RYKOV Shot	BUKHARIN Shot	SVERDLOV Dead	STALIN Survivor	ZINOVIEV Shot	KAMENEV Shot	TROTSKY In Exile	LENIN Dead
KOLLONTAI Missing?	URITSKY Dead	KRESTINSKY Shot	SMILGA Shot	NOGIN Dead	DZERZHINSKY Dead	BUBNOV Disappeared	SOKOLNIKOV In Prison
LOMOV ?	SHOMYAN Dead	BERZIN ?	MURANOV Disappeared	ARTEM Dead	STASSOVA Disappeared	MILIUTIN Missing	JOFFE Suicide

The Central Committee of The Bolshevik Party in 1917

◀ A picture published in an American newspaper by followers of Trotsky in the 1930s.

The purges spread to all levels of Soviet society. In 1937, Marshal Tuchachevsky, the commander-in-chief of the Red Army, and seven other generals were arrested. They were shot as spies without ever being brought to trial. By 1938, some 25,000 army officers had been purged. Millions of ordinary citizens had been arrested by the secret police.

The effects of the purges

By 1938, when Stalin relaxed his purges, there can have been few people brave enough to speak out against him. He had stamped out opposition very effectively. But he had also damaged Soviet industry and the army. Scientists, politicians, administrators, engineers and about two-thirds of the Red Army's officers had been executed or sent to labour camps.

The death of Trotsky

Trotsky, the man supposed to be behind all the plots against Stalin, was killed in Mexico in 1940 by one of Stalin's agents.

SUMMARY

Stalin's Purges – 1934

▶ Kirov assassinated.

▶ Stalin began purges of 'enemies of the state'.

▶ About 40,000,000 people arrested.

▶ Victims from all walks of life.

▶ Many victims confessed in show trials.

▶ Trotsky murdered in 1940.

ALLILUYEVA (1901–32)

Nadezhda Alliluyeva became Stalin's second wife in 1918. In 1921 the Party expelled her as a 'non-activist', but Stalin had her reinstated.

Alliluyeva was extremely concerned about the social costs of Stalin's policies. In 1932 she made a speech about the miseries that the Soviet people were suffering. The next day she committed suicide. Her death was a great embarrassment to Stalin.

CHAPTER 7

THE IMPACT OF THE SECOND WORLD WAR

The German threat

After Hitler came to power in Germany in January 1933, Stalin feared a German invasion. Hitler hated the Soviet people, calling them *Untermenschen* (sub-humans). He wanted to take the Soviet Union's oil and farmland. He also wanted Germans to run the Soviet Union, using Soviet people as slave labourers.

A change of heart?

But, in 1939, Germany and the Soviet Union signed the **Nazi-Soviet Pact**, agreeing not to fight each other. Neither side intended to stay allies. Hitler wanted to invade Poland without Soviet opposition. Stalin wanted to buy time to build up his troops, before the inevitable German attack.

7.1 Operation Barbarossa starts

In June 1941, Germany began **Operation Barbarossa** driving deep into the Soviet Union. The Soviet planes were destroyed by the German **Luftwaffe** (airforce).

Source **A**

▲ A British cartoon about the Nazi-Soviet Pact, published in 1939.

▼ The German invasion of the Soviet Union.

Countries occupied by or allied with Germany	▲▲▲▲▲ German start line, 1941
Soviet Union	▲▲▲▲▲ Furthest extent of German line
Neutral countries	Area taken by Germany but recaptured

German success

By the end of October 1941, German troops had destroyed 20,000 Soviet tanks and taken 2,000,000 prisoners. They had captured Kiev and were in sight of both Leningrad and Moscow.

Fighting the weather

The Germans had expected to defeat the Soviets before the worst of the winter took hold, but they did not. The Germans were unprepared for how fierce the winter was. Temperatures reached -35°C and soon more than 1,000,000 of the 3,000,000 German soldiers had frostbite. Oil froze in the tanks, and machine guns jammed. On 6 December, the Soviet General Zhukov attacked German troops who were advancing on Moscow. They were forced to abandon their advance.

Determined resistance

The Soviet villagers destroyed anything of value to the Germans (see Source B). The Germans were deep in Soviet territory and running very short of supplies. Yet when the spring came, Hitler ordered his troops to continue the advance. The main attacks were on Leningrad in the north and Stalingrad in the south. Leningrad had been besieged since September 1941. The siege lasted 900 days until 1944, when the Germans were finally defeated. The civilian people of the city had been reduced to eating cats, dogs, worms and even wallpaper glue. Almost 1,000,000 of them had died.

The battle for Stalingrad

In September 1942, two German armies advanced on Stalingrad. Hitler wanted the city to be taken at all costs. But Soviet resistance was equally determined, and the Germans had to fight for every house in every street.

In November 1942, the Soviets launched a counter-attack. They surrounded the Germans. Hitler told the German commander, Von Paulus, that he must not surrender under any circumstances. Von Paulus held out until January 1943, when he felt that his troops could not go on fighting. He surrendered and about 100,000 German soldiers were taken prisoner. A further 150,000 Germans had died trying to capture the city.

Source B

The enemy must not be left a single engine or railway truck. Collective farmers must drive off their cattle and turn their grain over to the State authorities. All property that cannot be carried away must be destroyed without fail.

In areas occupied by the enemy, secret groups must be organized to fight enemy units. Conditions must be made unbearable for the enemy.

▲ Part of a radio speech made by Stalin on 3 July 1941.

Source C

Soviet soldiers were very experienced in hand-to-hand fighting. They knew every drainpipe, manhole, shell-hole and crater in the city. Among the rubble, which no tanks could get through, the Soviet soldier turned on his machine gun as soon as a German was in firing range. Little short of a direct hit could knock him out.

▲ The Soviet general, Talensky, describes the heroism of Soviet troops defending Stalingrad in 1942.

Changing fortunes

The battle for Stalingrad was a turning point in the war. Hitler launched another attack in the summer of 1943, but was driven back. Hitler's invasion became a desperate retreat to Germany. By mid-1944, Soviet forces had driven the Germans out of the Soviet Union. In April 1945, Soviet troops entered the German capital, Berlin.

The cost of the war

Soviet victory in the war was a great boost to Stalin. He was a fine war-time leader. He had moved factories and raw materials to the Urals in 1941, where it was safe to make the equipment for the war. He also organized troops and supplies. But the war had been won at a huge cost. Over 20,000,000 Soviet citizens were killed. Huge areas of farmland and thousands of factories had been destroyed, as well as 70,000 villages and nearly 2,000 towns and cities. More Soviet people died defending Stalingrad than the United States lost in the whole war.

Evidence has recently been found that many Soviet people died in forced **deportation** (movement) by the Soviet government. Some areas, like the Ukraine and the Baltic States, welcomed the Germans as freeing them from Soviet rule. Stalin wanted to prevent other Soviet people from supporting the Germans. So he moved whole national groups (like the Chechens) to the east, where they could not work against the war effort. About 500,000 of them died in the process.

Source E

In March 1944, all the Chechen and Inguish people were deported. In April 1944, the Balkan people were sent to far away places.

The Ukrainians escaped only because there were too many of them and no place to send them. Otherwise Stalin would have deported them too.

▲ A speech made by Stalin's successor, Khrushchev, to the Communist Congress in Moscow in February 1956.

ZHUKOV (1896–1974)

Zhukov won many medals in the First World War. He fought for the Reds in the Civil War and was later sent to be trained as an officer at Frunze Military Academy in Moscow.

Zhukov was in charge of Soviet forces fighting the Japanese in Manchuria in 1939. During the Second World War he fought a famous campaign to save Moscow from the Nazis. He was promoted to Marshall. The Germans surrendered to him in Berlin in 1945.

Source D

◀ A Soviet poster from 1943 showing a young woman captured by the Germans. The words say: 'Our hope is in you, Red Warrior'. In the background, prisoners are being shot.

ВСЯ НАДЕЖДА НА ТЕБЯ, КРАСНЫЙ ВОИН!

An uneasy alliance

The Soviet Union, the United States and Britain had been allies against Germany, Italy and Japan in the war. But even before the war ended, it was clear they would not stay allies. Stalin felt the western powers would have liked Germany to overrun and weaken Russia because it was a communist country. After 1945, he made sure the Soviet Union was well defended against future attack.

Defence or attack?

The Red Army had freed much of eastern Europe from German occupation. But then Stalin took advantage of the fact that his army was in occupation to annex (take over) Estonia, Lithuania, Latvia, Finland and parts of Poland. He also made sure communist governments were elected in Czechoslovakia, Hungary, Poland, Bulgaria and Romania. Now the Soviet Union had a defensive 'buffer zone' between itself and the western powers.

The fears of the West

The western powers saw Stalin's actions differently. They believed the Soviet Union wanted to spread communism world-wide. They saw Stalin's actions as aggressive, not defensive. President Truman of the United States promised help to any country trying to stop communism.

The Cold War

In 1949, the United States and most of western Europe formed a military alliance called the **North Atlantic Treaty Organization (NATO)**. The Soviet Union promptly formed a communist alliance, the **Warsaw Pact**. For the next 40 years, the two sides kept up a **cold war**. This was a propaganda war in which east and west tried to discredit each other.

Source F

From Stettin on the Baltic to Trieste on the Adriatic, an iron curtain has descended across the continent.

Whatever conclusions may be drawn from these facts (and facts they certainly are), this is not the liberated Europe we fought to build up. Nor does it contain those things essential to permanent peace.

▲ Winston Churchill speaking at Fulton (USA) in March 1946.

▼ Soviet gains in eastern Europe 1945.

Soviet gains in eastern Europe 1945–9

NORWAY · FINLAND · SWEDEN · Estonia · Latvia · Lithuania · Stettin · GERMANY · Berlin · POLAND · FRANCE · CZECHOSLOVAKIA · SOVIET UNION · AUSTRIA · HUNGARY · ITALY · ROMANIA · YUGOSLAVIA · BULGARIA · ALBANIA · TURKEY

What did the Soviet people think of Stalin?

When Stalin died in March 1953, his body was put on display in the Kremlin. Thousands of Soviet citizens came to pay their last respects, and many wept in the street at the news of his death. But it is hard to find out what Soviet people really thought of Stalin. Many must have hated him, but could not say so. Criticism of Stalin was simply not allowed. The government had created a 'cult of Stalin'. There were pictures and statues of him all over the Soviet Union. Books, newspapers and films had to show him in a good light. Schools, hospitals and towns were named after him. Most of the criticism of Stalin from the time comes from foreign writers and artists.

Source 2

Soviet policeman: 'What do you think of the government, comrade?'
Soviet citizen (playing it very carefully): 'About the same as you do, comrade.'
Soviet policeman: 'In that case I've got to arrest you, comrade.'

▲ A joke from the Soviet Union during Stalin's leadership.

▼ A French cartoon from 1935. The caption says 'We are perfectly happy'.

Source 1

SOMMES BIEN HEUREUX

De-Stalinization

Nikita Khrushchev followed Stalin as Soviet leader in 1953. He made the first official criticisms of Stalin in a speech in 1956. This was followed by a policy of **de-Stalinization**. Stalin's economic policies were criticized. Political prisoners were released. Censorship was relaxed. There was a feeling that the Soviet Union was becoming more open minded.

Ordinary people

In chapters, 6 and 7 we have examined Stalin's most important policies. Many of them (the Five Year Plans, collectivization and Stalin's work during the war) can be used to criticize or praise Stalin. Other policies (the purges) obviously draw more criticism. But what about the day-to-day lives of ordinary Soviet people? They had to be careful about what they said. They were driven to meet high production targets. But how else did Stalin's rule affect them?

FACT FILE

1 Stalin insisted on free education. He said children needed education to be 'of the greatest possible service to the country'. By 1950, almost everyone between the ages of 8 and 50 could read and write.

2 Stalin would not allow divorce on request. He made abortion a crime. Large families were given tax benefits. Stalin wanted to increase the birth rate.

3 Many hospitals were built and thousands of doctors trained. The Soviet Union had more doctors per person than Britain. There was free health care for all.

4 Rebuilding and new housing projects started after the war. Flats in apartment blocks were provided for families, though there was still a housing shortage.

5 Russian workers were given paid holidays, insurance against accidents at work and retirement pensions.

6 The Orthodox Church had supported the government during the war. Stalin relaxed laws against religion. Thousands of churches were allowed to re-open.

Did the Soviet people gain from Stalin's rule?

The people of the Soviet Union had very little freedom under Stalin. His image appeared in the press and on almost every street corner. The message was hammered home that Comrade Stalin was the Soviet Union and the Soviet Union was Comrade Stalin. He could not be criticized. Opposition was ruthlessly suppressed. No one could properly assess Stalin's contribution to the Soviet Union under these conditions.

Stalin's successor, Khrushchev, denounced Stalin as a tyrant. Many historians now see him as ruthless and desperate to hang on to power. It is now unfashionable to see any good in Stalin's rule.

It is hoped that the sources on these pages, taken with Chapter 7, present a more balanced account of life in the Soviet Union under Stalin. You must make up your own mind about whether Stalin's rule benefited or harmed the people of the Soviet Union.

Source 3

Stalin was a very distrustful, suspicious man. He even distrusted Party workers he had known for years. He saw 'enemies', 'two-facers' and spies everywhere.

When Stalin said that someone should be arrested, it was necessary to accept on faith that he was an 'enemy of the people'. From 1954 to the present time, the military section of the Supreme Court has cleared the names of 7,679 persons, many of whom were dead.

Stalin glorified himself. He tried to convince people that all the Soviet victories in the war were due to his courage, daring and genius – and no-one else.

It was not Stalin, but the Party as a whole, the Soviet government, our heroic army, its talented leaders and soldiers, the whole Soviet nation – who won victory in the war.

Comrades! We must abolish the cult of Stalin once and for all.

▲ Extracts from a speech made by Khrushchev to the Communist Party's Twentieth Congress in 1956.

INDEX